Living Faithfully in the Age of Terror

Brief Devotionals Based on the Judeo-Christian Tradition

by

Henry C. Blount, Jr. D. Min

D1295902

DORRANCE
PUBLISHING CO
EST. 1920
PITTSBURGH, PENNSYLVANIA 15238

The contents of this work, including, but not limited to, the accuracy of events, people, and places depicted; opinions expressed; permission to use previously published materials included; and any advice given or actions advocated are solely the responsibility of the author, who assumes all liability for said work and indemnifies the publisher against any claims stemming from publication of the work.

Dorrance Publishing Co
585 Alpha Drive Suite 103
Pittsburgh, PA 15238
Visit our website at *www.dorrancebookstore.com*

ISBN: 978-1-4809-1132-1
eISBN: 978-1-4809-1454-4

TABLE OF CONTENTS

1. Living Faithfully in the Age of Terror 1
2. Take the high road 3
3. Who's poking holes in my ark? 5
4. Life is a school-your class is in session 7
5. You are contagious 9
6. Thumping watermelons 11
7. Too many "old" people 13
8. Who's on your front row? 15
9. Trying to spell God with the "right" blocks 17
10. The silent beating of the drums 20
11. Wisdom from a sandbox 22
12. Need a personality make-over? 24
14. Slow me down, Lord 27
15. The healing art of listening 29
16. The time of your life...is now 31
17. Real role models 33
18. Interruptions can be a blessing 35
19. Love has its own language 37
20. The art of being wrong 39
21. Let the river take you 41
22. Don't rock the boat 43
23. Beatitudes for fathers and other imperfect people 45
24. A faith worth having 47
25. When God comes into focus 49
26. The most important word 51
27. When your faith is tested 53
28. Are you struggling with your faith? 55
29. Everyone needs a little help 57
30. Peak experiences 59

31. Who stole my buggy?...61
32. Beyond the blues...63
33. Worried sick and sick of worrying...64
34. Your soul is a work in progress 66
35. Happiness without guilt 68
36. Negative thinking can pull you down—way down...........................70
37. A little religion is a dangerous thing 72
38. Ways to wrinkle your soul..74
39. God writes straight with crooked lines....................................76
40. Dealing with demons 78
41. Coping with loss 80
42. Making peace with our passages 82
43. When life is a drag, you do have the power to cope!....................85
44. If I've got it made, why am I so miserable?..............................88
45. Living a quality life...90
46. You are chosen..92
47. Why do we suffer?...94
48. Finding heaven in the here and now 96
49. Born Again Perfume..98
50. How can we be content in a world like this?............................101
51. Lost in your own backyard...103
52. Are you out of your mind? 105
53. Some assembly required 107
54. Sex is a sacred trust..109
55. It's your family—for better or worse....................................112
56. I do windows 114
57. A case for compassion 116
58. The "yin and yang" of our faith...118
59. The destructive power of judging 120
60. Hypocrites in the church? No way...122
61. Grace is more than a blue-eyed blonde...................................124
62. Don't lose your joy..126
63. The road less graveled...128
64. Love like you've never been hurt 130
65. Is death a dirty joke?..132
66. "Sweet are the uses of adversity"...134
67. Writing your own epitaph 136
68. Love heals when nothing else will..138
69. Enjoying the second half of life (Part I) 140
70. Enjoying the second half of life (Part II)................................143
71. What's it like being a preacher?...146
72. Keeping centered—keeping sane..148
73. Happiness is only real when shared..151

INTRODUCTION

In a sense, the material in this book has been incubating for at least a half century. It is the result of research for sermons delivered throughout the Louisiana Annual Conference as well as columns written for the Cen-La Focus, a lifestyle publication in Alexandria, Louisiana, where I retired as a Methodist Minister in 1992.

I've had a varied background, not only preaching but teaching in four Louisiana Universities, La Tech in Ruston, LSU in Baton Rouge, Northwestern in Natchitoches, and Alexandria Division of Upper Iowa University. Subjects taught were Marriage and The Family, Social Problems, Human Development, World Religions, Philosophy, and Biblical Literature. I've also taught Pastoral Care and Counseling for Seminary students at the Shreveport Division of Drew Theological Seminary, New Jersey. I hold a B.A. degree from Millsaps College in Jackson, Mississippi; M. Div. from Emory University in Atlanta, Georgia, and a D. Min from the Iliff School of Theology in Denver, Colorado.

I worked in a privately owned psychiatric hospital in Alexandria, as a day therapist for two years following my first retirement.

I have drawn from all of these disciplines, as well as a study in Zen Buddhism and other Eastern philosophies. I don't like labels because I am liberal about some issues, conservative about others. I refuse to be put in a theological box, for my Christian faith is dynamic and I am open to truth wherever I find it. I find it impossible to be a practicing Christian and not be influenced by other philosophical and religious disciplines. My heroes of the faith include Martin Buber, Karl Barth, Paul Tillich, John Wesley, Martin Luther, Carl Yung, Thomas Merton, Martin Luther King, C.S. Lewis, Dietrich Bonhoeffer, David McIntosh, Richard Rohr, Edgar Cayce, the Jesuits and many others.

I believe very strongly in what some Wesleyan scholars have called the "Optimism of Grace." I believe God is ever-present in human beings, and I am interested in the way God works through personalities. A friend commented that I will have to be reincarnated as a fundamentalist to work through my karma. I believe fundamentalism misses the rich mysteries of our faith, although I would stand up for their right to freedom of belief.

My faith in not "pollyanna-ish," for I do recognize the power and devastation of evil in the world, especially since 9/11. I have dedicated my life to Christ and I will try to promote the spirit of *agape* love as long as I am able. I am an incurable optimist.

I believe salvation is not just something we do. It is something that is done to us when we become free of all prejudices, judgments, labels and hatred. We must empty ourselves for God's love to fill us.

My personal motto is NEVER STUMBLE ON ANYTHING BEHIND YOU. I have tried to encourage people to keep praying, witnessing, and taking a stand for what is good, true and beautiful, and live by the positive and Godly teachings of the Old and New Testaments. I believe this is our greatest hope for the twenty-first century. As someone has said: "The safest place in the world is in the center of God's Love."

ABOUT THE AUTHOR

Henry C. Blount, Jr. is a retired United Methodist Minister living in Alexandria, LA with his wife, Joann. He retired in 1992 from the First United Methodist Church in Alexandria and was named Pastor Emeritus in 2013. He has served churches throughout Louisiana.

Blount is the father of three daughters and two sons, eleven grandchildren and eight great-grandchildren. His first wife, Marilyn died in 2006 of Alzheimer's disease.

Besides being a columnist for the Cen-La Focus, he is also a watercolorist, having studied under Doug Walton of Ruston, Louisiana.

He is a veteran of World War II, having served as a Radio Technician on a Destroyer Escort in the North Atlantic.

He is the author of two previous publications, <u>Looking For Honey</u> and <u>Soul Sounds,</u> published by Land and Land Publishers in Baton Rouge, Louisiana. He is also a football fan of LSU in Baton Rouge, and the New Orleans' Saints, a daily swimmer and an avid gardener.

ACKNOWLEDGMENTS

This book has been an ongoing project for several decades due to the privilege of serving wonderful congregations throughout the Louisiana United Methodist Conference as the senior minister. It would have been impossible without the encouragement of so many.

Also it would never have been printed without Mr. Willie Harp and son, Will, editors and publishers of the Cen-La Focus, a life-style publication for Central Louisiana. I will always be grateful for their willingness to include my column in the monthly Cen-La Focus for over a decade. Most of the material in this book came from those columns.

And then, I am grateful to God for the ability and energy to have this book published. I've been tempted at times to discard this project and sit on the back porch, but something kept me coming back to the computer. I hope you will be blessed by it.

Henry C. Blount, Jr.
Alexandria, La.

Dr. Blount has been an integral part of our magazine's success over the last decade. His insightful spiritual and life advice serve as the cornerstone of our very popular "Faith Focus" section each month. Highly anticipated each month, Dr. Blount brings a sometime humorous, and always positive messages to our readership with every article.
- Willie Harp and son Will,
Editors and Publishers of Cenla Focus

DEDICATION

This book is lovingly dedicated to my patient wife, Joann Collins Blount, who is giving me a "second chance to wholeness."

It is also dedicated to the memory of all who are victims of terrorism.

LIVING FAITHFULLY
IN THE AGE OF TERROR

I remember the first time the word "faith" came into focus for me. I had joined the Navy and was serving as a Radar Technician on a Destroyer Escort, searching for "enemy" submarines. It was far more dangerous than I realized at the time. Each letter I received from home ended with these words: "Have faith." I didn't know exactly what that meant so I talked with the Chaplain. He said that faith was no assurance that I would get home safe and sound, but I needed to trust God, and pray daily, regardless of the outcome.

So I realized that "faith" is not some kind of insurance policy against the dangers of life. I believe that's the way it is in today's world, which (as we know) is full of a variety of dangers. "The rain falls on the just and the unjust." (Matthew 5:45)

Someone may ask, where was God during the Boston Marathon Bombing? It's clear to me that God was in the hearts of those who rushed to the people who were suffering - those who risked their lives; those who value the sacredness of life. The two brothers had apparently rejected this belief and were following a destructive path.

The Rev. Gerald Mann has a book, Common Sense Religion, in which he writes, "There's a yes in every mess." The Apostle Paul wrote to the Corinthians (II Cor.1:20) "For all the promises of God find their "Yes" in Christ. That is why we say "Amen" through him" (II Cor.1:20) These words were written to the congregation in Corinth, people who were fighting among themselves and were guilty of lying, adultery and abusing Holy Communion. So Paul talked about love as the greatest power in the world.

If you are like me, you are looking for the "yes" in the world's mess today. We have lived in the age of anxiety, age of industry, age of terror, and now there's talk about "the nuclear age." This would probably be the greatest mess

1

of all. Frankly I doubt that any one in their right mind would start a nuclear war. "In their right mind" is a big assumption.

Finding something positive in every negative situation is a big job. I don't have any pat answers or easy clichés, but I do remind myself of certain positive thoughts in order to keep my perspective. (I almost said "keep my sanity" but that may be asking too much.) Joann and I were coming back from Lake Charles recently, and my car had a blow-out flat. The car right behind us stopped and a man, Rob Landry from Praireville, got out and asked us if we needed help. In just a few minutes, we were back on the road again, thanks to a "Good Samaritan." This is just a small illustration that there are people out there, everywhere, who are willing to go out of their way to help others. People like Rob Landry help me keep my balance in a broken world.

I need to be reminded that Jesus lived in a terrifying time, but there were Good Samaritans in his day too. But he was not exempt, nor are we, from murderers and "those who break through and steal." His post-resurrection message to His Disciples was not to go back and zap it to the Romans. However unpopular it might have been then, and even now, he asked them to "pray for those who abused them, and to love their enemies." He was not trying to win a popularity contest, but simply to show that love is better than hatred, and that it is better to pray for your enemies than to kill them.

The Jesus ethic has never really caught on. I don't believe it is pre-destined but there are wars and rumors of war, and war in some form is likely to continue across the human landscape, as long as there are people who are different from each other. The sad part is the fact that religion plays a major role. We need to keep praying for unity in the midst of diversity.

PRAYER: Dear Lord: Thank you for the gift of life, but Lord we need Your help. I know you have given us freedom of choice, so forgive us abusing this gift and making destructive choices. Touch the hearts of those who feel that they must kill if others don't believe as they do. I give thanks for the millions upon millions of good people who are honest, hard-working citizens, and who are trying to make life better for all of us. Help us to live and let live and to be decent in our deeds, and compassionate in our dealings. When we are driven to our knees, help us to know that's a good time to pray. Please give us the strength of mind and heart to live faithfully no matter what happens. May we ask "what is the loving thing to do?" in all circumstances. And by all means, help us to celebrate the good and beautiful things in life. In the name of Jesus. Amen.

Carve out a time (at least 30 minutes) a day for solitude, reflection and prayer.

TAKE THE HIGH ROAD

I enjoy "people watching." It's almost as interesting as bird watching. It's fascinating to sit on a bench in the mall and watch different people go by, especially little plump babies in pink baby buggies. What a variety God has created. I also like to see how people respond to different situations. Sometimes I see things that inspire me, like older couples walking, holding hands. But I also see things that are bothersome, like the woman who slaps her little boy for crying. He just cries louder. What did she expect?

In my counseling experiences, I often tell people to "take the high road." Try to do the right thing, even though you may be criticized or ostracized. Even though life may slap you around. Swallow your pride and forgive the other person even though they didn't ask for forgiveness. You are taking the high road when you can put negative experiences in the past and move on. Or when you become non-judgmental and realize that judging is not your calling. You are taking the high road when you stop confessing the other person's sin, and work on your own short comings. Of course, it's difficult to always take the high road. Sometimes we want to even the score, or hold on to our wounds. It can be an eye-for-an-eye kind of thing.

In Robert Frost's poem "The Road Less Traveled," Frost talks about two roads that diverge in the woods and how he took the one less traveled by. It must have been the high road, where folks put their best foot forward, and are positive and forgiving without holding grudges.

Jesus of Nazareth was always taking the high road, even though it was the roughest road around. He wanted to do the right thing, to do God's will if you please, not that he pleased the obnoxiously religious Pharisees or the other rigid law-keepers of that day. He healed a man on the Sabbath, which to us seems pretty compassionate, but this was against their silly rules. Some play by their own senseless rules.

When Jesus said do unto others as you would have them do unto you, he was guiding them to a higher road. Respect others as you want to be respected. Love people who are difficult to love. Stop judging. Go the second mile.

Is Jesus asking that we give up our boundaries? Or that we throw all rules out the window? Of course not. Some rules serve a good purpose. He was asking us to be creative, innovative and not stoop to the same level as those who hurt us, or hate us.

So look at yourself and ask what it means for you to take the high road. It could mean a change of habits, or giving up negative attitudes, or making an apology, or praying for the ones who are the most difficult to pray for. It may mean realizing that you are a child of God, created in His Spiritual Image, and that you deserve to be at peace with the world around you even in the midst of turmoil. It could mean that won't get your nose out of joint when you have to stand in long lines, or get caught in a traffic snarl, or when one of the kitchen pipes burst. It may mean telling those who are closest to you that you love them - and doing this every day, even though they may not deserve it sometimes.

Taking the high road means to stop feeling sorry for yourself, and leading with your strength and not your weakness. It's letting God lead you to a happier place. The high road is full of them. Amen.

WHO'S POKING HOLES
IN MY ARK?

Every now and then, something clever shows up on the Internet. Such was the case recently with a picture of Noah's Ark, full of animals, two-of-a-kind, of course. But lo and behold, at the bow of the ship was a red-headed woodpecker chipping away, poking holes in the side of the vessel. Those on the ship looked very anxious and Noah was trying to throw a net around the bird before it was too late.

Isn't this a parable for us today? We have our arks neatly arranged. Life is going along fine, blessings come in bundles, but there always seem to be "woodpeckers" around, poking holes in our security, frustrating us with political shenanigans, trying to destroy our happiness and well-being, threatening to scare us or to annihilate us altogether.

I've wondered what the Apostle Paul in the New Testament had in mind when he wrote to the Corinthians that he had a "thorn in the flesh." (See II Cor.7-10) It could have been a chronic illness or someone who irritated him, or poor vision (he did have a blinding experience on the road to Damascus). Whatever it was, Paul's Ark seemed to be under constant attack.

What about you? Is something or someone trying to poke holes in YOUR ark? My mama used to say, "There's always something..." Truly there is. To paraphrase Jesus (John 16:33): "In this world you will have "woodpeckers," but be of good cheer, I have overcome the world."

Come to think of it, I can do a rather thorough job of poking holes in my own ark. I can allow my mind to settle on negative thoughts of impending doom, and worry needlessly, as if worry will change things. I can be my own worst enemy in the poor choices I make. I can bring misery to my own backdoor when fail to see life through the eyes of faith.

And to be sure, others can poke holes in our "arks." In our world today, we meet all kinds, some wonderful and some not so wonderful. Someone gave me this prayer: "God grant me the good fortune to avoid people I never liked, the good fortune to run into the ones I do, and the eyesight to see the difference."

There's another dimension to all of this. The "woodpecker" can also be the suffering that comes just because we're human. Is there ever any real security in this life? Being human has always been hazardous to our health. Some of us get diseases, lose our jobs, lose loved ones, lose our mind, try to dodge natural disasters and experience a vast assortment of headaches and difficulty: mentally, physically and emotionally.

When tragedy hits or when the crisis comes our way, we may ask, out of our frustration and grief, "Why me?" Where is God in all of this? If God is good why did God allow it? If God is all-powerful, why didn't God prevent it?"

It seems to me that WHY is not the appropriate question, but rather HOW? How can I make it through the night? What can I learn from this? How can I cope with this situation without losing my basic trust in the goodness of God? Somehow I need a faith that allows for joy in the midst of suffering. That may not make much sense to some. The kind of joy I'm talking about is hearing the small still, voice say, "Peace, be still," during all the storms of life.

Philip Yancey tells about a nurse in a hospice who described the results of faith evident at the bedside of dying patients. "I see a difference in how families with faith handle death. They mourn, of course, and cry, but they also hug each other and pray and sing hymns. There's less terror. For those without faith, death is final. It ends everything. They stand around and talk about the past. People with faith remind each other there will also be a future." (Reaching For An Invisible God, p.21)

So, as long as we are in these physical bodies, we will face the unwanted and unexpected "pecking" as well as the inevitable passages of life. And let us not forget that all of us are in the SAME ark. All of us have basically the same challenges in life, so let's be good to each other and keep the ark as safe as we can. Amen.

Forgive everyone for everything.

LIFE IS A SCHOOL-
YOUR CLASS IS IN SESSION

Life is indeed a school and the minute you were born, your class was in session.

I thought about this the other day while visiting a friend. She was having a rough time, one burden or crisis after another, it seemed. "I suppose all of us are entitled to our own problems," she said, "or we wouldn't learn or grow spiritually."

Her point is well taken, but sometimes I wonder what possible lesson or growth could come out of certain situations. After my second heart by-pass surgery, I thought, "Lord, how much spiritual growth do I need? I mean, isn't there a cut-off somewhere?"

So many lessons come from mistakes, poor choices, and (dare I say it?) sin. I know a man who has been divorced 5 times. Slow learner.

After I heard the following story, I couldn't resist passing it along.

There was a family of wayward church members, a father and three sons who once were active in their church. The preacher visited them often but to no avail. One day a rattlesnake bit the youngest son, John. The doctor came and pronounced his condition grave. The father quickly sent for the preacher to come and pray for John's recovery. This was his prayer:

"Oh wise Heavenly Father, we thank thee that thou hast, in thy wisdom, sent a rattlesnake to bite John, to bring him to his senses. He promised to become active in his church again. And now Father, wilt thou send another rattlesnake to bite Sam and one to bite Jim and one to bite the old man. It seems that what I couldn't do, Thou hast done by sending a rattlesnake, so Lord, please send bigger and better ones soon. I thank Thee. Amen."

Seriously folks, people do seem to grow a lot when faced with their own mortality, snake bite or whatever. When a big life-threatening crisis comes along, most of us would welcome a few prayers.

Some believe that God sends trouble to sinners as "divine punishment." In the Old Testament, a man named Job lost everything he had. His so-called friends pointed out that his sins had brought on these catastrophes. But Job won the battle and said: "Though He slay me, yet will I trust Him." (Job 13:15) Nothing could destroy Job's faith.

The Greek philosopher Plato, in his *Dialogues*, wrote about healing the body by healing the spirit, or soul. We must deal with our past, with our sins, or we go on punishing ourselves. According to Plato, it is through art and love that God breaks through to us.

Or consider the lessons that came from Jesus of Nazareth. Medicine not only owes a great deal to people like Plato and Hippocrates, but also to Jesus. It was the humble Galilean who, more than any other historical figure, bequeathed to the healing arts their basic meaning and spirit. The lessons Jesus gave were based on unselfish love, and physicians would do well to remind themselves that without compassionate love, medicine degenerates into depersonalized methodology. Amen.

YOU ARE CONTAGIOUS

It was a bumpy flight all the way from Baton Rouge to Atlanta.

My friend Barry and I were en route to a meeting. I was sitting next to the window, Barry was in the middle and a stranger was on the aisle seat. Assuming that the stranger didn't like to fly, I leaned over to Barry and whispered, "The guy next to you is wringing his hands and seems very uptight. You're a Christian, so encourage him a little." In a few moments, I heard Barry ask him, "Is this your first flight?"

"Oh no, not at all," he said, "I'm an airplane mechanic and I know how easy these things can fall apart," and he commenced making a whirling motion and a crashing vocal sound. Barry leaned over to me and said: "HE's making ME nervous." "Yeah, I know what you mean." I laughed under my breath (a little).

Of course, we ARE contagious. People CAN make us nervous. You can be around certain people for five minutes and get a head-ache - no doubt about it, we rub off on others. Psychologists tell us that we actually become a part of everything that happens to us. The things we see, hear and do become integrated into our personalities, however minor they may be.

This is the reason we warn our children to be careful who they run around with. I can just hear my momma's warning, "the birds of a feather flock together," or, "monkey see, monkey do." It occurs to me that maybe THEIR parents are warning their kids not to associate with ours either.

When the church was beginning to take shape in the first century, as recorded in the Book of Acts, there is a reference to the boldness of Peter and John who couldn't help but speak the things they had seen and heard. This is how others "recognized that they had been with Jesus." (Acts 4:13-17) Certain spiritual qualities had rubbed off on them, and the Christian movement began to take shape.

That movement exists today because people have continued to rub off on each other.

Think of the people who've influenced you, those who have had the greatest impact on your values and behavior. It may be your mama, or daddy, or Sunday school teacher, or coach or whoever. We may say to ourselves, "I want what that person has," or, "I would like to have her outlook on life," or, "I want to be like him." One human being inspiring and helping another human being keeps the world turning and makes life worth living. It's the network behind every civilization.

There is a ceremony in our church tradition which illustrates this very well. Older, retiring ministers pass the mantle (a liturgical stole) on to the younger ministers during the Ordination Service. It's a beautiful way to symbolize the way we influence and encourage those who will come after us, who follow the path left by those gone before us. The symbol of our faith is handed down from one generation to the other.

One of the ongoing dangers of the church is that we can be so busy tending to our buildings, the upkeep of property, etc., that we lose sight of the individual. We can be so focused on the mechanics of a worship service that we are blind to woman grieving the loss of her husband, the man who has a depressive disorder, the young person who is struggling with sexuality. We can be so busy going to church meetings that we don't hear the cry of loneliness from those in nursing homes, or half-way houses, or hospitals, or other places where people are suffering silently. It's a good thing to protect our institutions, but not to allow ourselves to become insensitive to individual needs.

The church has a tremendous challenge in today's world. Television, movies, the Internet, and so on are causing a major value-shift on our morals and ethics, and almost every aspect of human behavior. We are challenged like never before to uphold the values that help individuals to have self-respect, to respect others and to live a life that's helpful and decent, a life that makes a difference, a life that cares about all of God's creation.

The people who are most helpful to me are not those who buttonhole you and try to talk you into believing a certain way, but those who live their lives gracefully, kindly, and are involved in helping to make this a better world.

May their tribe increase.

> Express love every day to those in your life. All that matters in the end is the faith you have and the love you've expressed.

THUMPING WATERMELONS

I was in a grocery store the other day, tending to my own shopping spree, when my eyes fell upon a bin of watermelons. I leaned over to thump one, then another and another, when a voice next to me said, "Sir, I've watched you thump those melons. Would you tell me what you're listening for?"

I began giving her a "thumping" demonstration, and when two other people gathered around to hear, I said in my most authoritative voice, "When you thump a melon, you don't want to hear a 'thud' because a hard sound means it's too green. A ripe melon has a soft, mellow sound." Then they began thumping for themselves, and finally bought a melon with the right sound. I couldn't help offering a little prayer: "Lord, help those melons to be ripe." (I'm glad I didn't leave them my name.)

This is a parable on the way we live our lives by faith. When life opens up for us, we don't know exactly what's in store. I have it on the authority of Forest Gump, who quoted his mother about life being like a box of chocolates, not knowing what you're going to get.

Life is lived by faith. You could hardly get through a single day without exercising your faith that what you're eating or taking from a bottle, won't kill you.

When we look at our religious faith, the same principle applies. I have faith that God is real and is the sole (soul) power behind this universe, but I don't always know what will happen because of it. I believe that God is to be trusted and will give strength and comfort to those who need it most. This may come as a surprise or revelation. From the time a doctor "thumps" our bottom until the time we exit life, there is a mystery and uncertainty and we never know what a day will bring. But having a vital faith in the ultimate goodness of God somehow helps me to face whatever happens.

There must be many people like the man who said to Horace Greeley one day, "I am a self-made man." "Good," said Greeley, "that relieves God of a terrible responsibility."

I've learned that it is pointless to argue about religion. A religious faith is so personal and emotionally charged that few people change their mind through arguments. A personal faith is not built on how many times we go to church (although that may help). Our faith is directly related to the way we treat each other, and how we us our God-given talents.

Sometimes, people confuse faith with an "insurance policy." If God is real, they say, then why do the innocent suffer, or why do tornadoes, hurricanes, etc. kill at random? If God is all-powerful, why doesn't God do something about the evil in our world?

These are hard questions without easy answers, but is there anything that says any of us will escape harm, suffering, illness, disease, or death? God simply doesn't give insurance policies against pain. The "dash" between our birth date and death date represents a great mixture of pain and pleasure, joy and sadness, rewards and regrets.

I've heard the comment that evolution has taken God's place. I see no conflict here. The truth of evolution is God's truth. God, to me, is still is in the assembly line of creation, and every truth of science traces the footsteps of God.

So, I will go on thumping "summer's sacred fruit," not knowing exactly what's inside. And I will still have faith that the next one will be a little sweeter than the last one, just as I have faith that tomorrow will be a little better than today. Amen.

TOO MANY "OLD" PEOPLE

Yep, you read it right, too many "old" people in this country. I don't mean chronologically, but emotionally, old attitudes, old prejudices and people who forget how to have fun.

It's easy to lose your sense of wonder, and to take yourself too seriously. And then worry about everything, carrying the weight of the world of your shoulders.

Jesus put it this way: "You must become as little children to enter the Kingdom of God." The Disciples had been arguing about who is the greatest in the Kingdom, and Jesus took the hand of a child and said, "Unless you humble yourself as this child, you will never enter the Kingdom of Heaven."

Children are not always little angels. They can be noisy, selfish and demanding. Turn them loose and they can be a wrecking crew.

But there are certain characteristics that make them special. There is usually a lack of phoniness in kids. They tend to be open and honest with no hidden agendas.

I was visiting a family one day who had been absent from church lately. As we sat in the living room, the mother said, "We go to my home town in Arkansas just about every weekend, and we go to church there." Her 6 or 7 year-old son said, "Mama, we don't go to church there." I changed the subject. I don't badger people about attending worship services anyway.

Blessed are those who are honest, who tell it like it is.

Kids have fun and it seems to come naturally. They tend to enjoy life. They don't waste time "waiting" for things to change. If it rains, they play in it. If it's hot, they turn on the water hose. A child doesn't feel guilty until we teach them how. They don't know how to worry until they learn it from adults. A child can laugh at the least thing, and can have a ball with the most unlikely toys. There is a spontaneous joy in kids that's contagious.

The late Roscoe Bolton is prime example here. During his funeral, one of his grandsons referred to "Bepop" as one who loved to dance, eat good food, laugh and so on. Roscoe, though 99, had a young heart. The "kid" in him was alive and well.

I have it on the authority of Dr. Chris Thacker, senior pastor of Alexandria, Emmanuel Baptist Church, who pointed out in a sermon recently that faith and fun are considered the "odd" couple. Faith doesn't know what to do with fun. We say "Christian can have fun too," but we say it almost apologetically, as if it's the exception to the rule for Christians to have a good time.

Jesus also used the word "humility" in reference to children. Humility is a rare virtue in our society. We admire those who are aggressive, assertive, and those who are go-getters.

When Pope Pius IX was elected pope, he became arrogant, pompous and impressed with his own importance. Shortly after the election, he allowed his Mother to come to see him. He held up his ring and said, "With this ring, I will rule the world." His mother smiled, as she held up her wedding ring and said, "Without this ring, you wouldn't be here in the first place."

Humility is not being a doormat. It is not bowing down to evil just to keep peace. It is putting yourself in the other person's place and being sensitive to his or her needs. It is recognizing the needs of others. Jesus didn't talk about humility. He lived it. One day, he laid aside his garments, took a towel and water and began washing the feet of his disciples.

It seems that most people live "outside" themselves. Our society is "outer-directed" as we are caught up in busyness, a thirst for possessions, speed, conquest, and instant gratification. We live on the outside of the spiritual self, therefore we can become spiritually bankrupt. A child is "inner-directed," and speaks from the heart.

So, we need to celebrate the child that is within each of us. As Paul Tillich once said, "The nature of salvation is the nature of a child."

I close with the words of Michael Quoist, who has included the following in his book on prayer. "God says I like youngsters, I want people to be like them. I don't like old people unless they are still children. I only want children in my kingdom—Youngsters who are twisted, humped, wrinkled, and white bearded. I like little children, because my image has not been dulled in them...I like them because they are still growing, they are still improving."

Go out-of-doors EVERYDAY, and notice the formation of clouds, trees, sunsets, flowers, etc., and thank God for so many free gifts.

WHO'S ON YOUR FRONT ROW?

At a recent weekend retreat, a friend handed me a piece of paper with this message:

> "Life is a theatre, so choose your audience carefully.
> Some people are not healthy enough to be that close.
> And you have to love some people from a distance.
> So, be careful who you allow on your front row."

At first, this quote struck me as rather snobbish or self-righteous. The New Testament tells us that Jesus ate with sinners and the down-and-outers. On second thought, however, I can see the value in such a statement.

There are many good people but some are negative and draining and you can be around them twenty minutes and feel bad. It has everything to do with the quality of good or poor relationships.

Now, let me try to describe those I'd like to have on my front row.

It would be better, first of all, to have *encouragers* rather than *discouragers*. There are people who offer words of hope; they have an easy smile and a loving spirit. I feel good in their presence. My front row would be full of those who offer life-lines of joy and optimism. They take the *high road*.

I'd rather have *non-complainers* on my front row than those who are prone to complain and criticize. Complaining and labeling seems to be a favorite past-time for many who have nothing more interesting to do.

Of course, there are times when all of us may have something legitimate to complain about. If I have a toothache, I am not going to sing "It's a Wonderful World." So my reference here is about the habitual complainer or criticizer: "Nothing is ever right," "It's their fault," "Nobody knows the trouble I've seen," "The world is going down the drain," etc. These are people who seldom find encouraging words about anything.

My front row would certainly include those who have a *good sense of humor*. I tend to stay away from those who have soured on life and seek out those who can laugh at themselves, whatever the circumstances happen to be. When we can't poke fun at ourselves, and when we don't allow others to do so, it's probably because we are trying to protect the dark side of our persona.

So, observe the relationships around you. Notice the ones that *lift* and the ones that *lean*. When you leave certain people, do you feel better or worse? Which ones seem always to have a drama going full speed, and which ones seem to enjoy inner peace?

We cannot change the people around us, but we can *change* the people we are around.

We can love them from the balcony. Amen.

TRYING TO SPELL GOD
WITH THE "RIGHT" BLOCKS

"The world is a spiritual kindergarten in which millions of bewildered infants are trying to spell God with the wrong blocks." (Anonymous)

Down through the ages, people have debated, meditated, cogitated, and ruminated over a belief in God. Questions keep us inquisitive. Where is God? What kind of power does God have? How does God interact with life on this planet? Is God personally concerned about our welfare and destiny? We want to know why and how the world was made. We crave knowledge, anything that makes sense.

This reminds me of what Thomas Jefferson did when he was the president. He re-wrote the New Testament to suit his beliefs. He didn't change the words, he just left out a lot of things he couldn't understand, such the miracles and references to the supernatural. (See *Thomas Jefferson: The Art of Power* by Jon Meacham. Random House, 2012, p. xxi)

God is much more than any WORD that we use to describe God. God defies explanation, and easy answers. And we don't really know what to do with Evolution, the Big Bang theory and the Book of Genesis. (Genesis tells us WHY the world was created, not HOW.) I believe that science traces the "footsteps" of God. I see no contradiction between science and religion.

I have listened to televangelists who portray an immature belief system, one that imagines a "slot machine" God: push in a prayer and pull out a favorable answer. I realize that this sounds a little judgmental, but I believe such descriptions are fraudulent. On the other hand, God is more than some intellectual theory.

Theologians tell us that there are five major arguments for God.

1. Cosmological: The cosmos could not have created itself.
2. Teleological: The world has purpose, and behind the Universe is Master Designer.

3. Ontological: God is "BEING," whose very nature implies existence. Theologian Paul Tillich declared that "God is the ground of our Being."
4. Moral: There is a universal urge to do the right thing, based on values of an Absolute Mind.
5. Christological: The life and teachings of Jesus of Nazareth.

I agree with all of the above, but theories don't do a lot for me. They are forerunners of dogma and dogmas limit the human mind. In other words, a person who is dogmatic has all the information they need, period. No room for growth or change. Furthermore, God is to be experienced and not theorized.

There are other synonyms for God: Creator, Lover, Higher Power, Law Giver, Father, Mother, Redeemer, and others - but as I say, no word can capture the full meaning of Deity.

The real issue, it seems to me, is not THAT we believe in God, but WHAT do we believe ABOUT God? For example there is a boat. I can see it and touch it. It exists. BUT I am not about to get on it and have a personal relationship with it. My belief then is purely intellectual and nothing more. Some say they believe in God or a Higher Power but that's as far as it goes.

Jesus gives us a far more personal God when He called Him "Our Father. Abba." In fact The Lord's Prayer reflects a lot about God, and is said to be a summary of the Gospel. Jesus said, when you pray, say "Our Father." The word *our* Father implies that God is the God for all of us, not just a select few. And yet, many people are spelling God with hatred, vengeance, retaliation, bombs, and now there is talk of one country using chemical weapons. The way to spell God has always been "love," forgiveness and redemption.

"Thy Kingdom come, Thy will be done, on Earth as it is in Heaven." Heaven begins now. The Kingdom is not in some far away future. We are living in the Kingdom. There's an old story about a man who raised roses as a hobby, and once a friend said, "You and God have made something beautiful here." But the man answered, "You should have seen it when God had it by Himself." Thus, we are co-creators with God. I think about this when I look into the face of a new-born baby. It's Creation all over again.

"Give us this day our daily bread." Note that Jesus said OUR, not MY bread. Those of us who have bread need to be ever aware of those without bread, and do what we can to feed the poor and under-privileged. There are so many needy people in the world, and it's easy to resist so many requests for money for starving children, etc. I wish I could send money to all of them, but I have to be selective. They pull at your heart-strings. Some have proven fraudulent, but there are many legitimate needy causes.

"Lead us not into temptation." It is not God who leads us, but we put ourselves in a vulnerable position. We are easily tempted, and we eat the forbidden fruit. We call upon God to help us to turn away from anything that is destructive. We are praying for protection when we pray, "Deliver us from evil." We exercise freedom of choice constantly.

The ending of the Lord's Prayer, "For Thine is the Kingdom and the power and the glory forever," was actually an addition which the church added to make it appropriate for a liturgy. But it's in harmony with the thoughts of Jesus.

So this brief prayer voices our need for communion with our Heavenly Father, a prayer for God's will to be done throughout the world. It lifts us to an optimistic faith in God, the Creator.

Sometimes I think about my mother's faith, which was short and simple. When matters of religion would come up for discussion, she would always quote Romans 8:28, "We know that all things work together for good for those who love God, who are called according to His purpose." Can God be "spelled" any better than that?

THE SILENT BEATING
OF THE DRUMS

If you've ever felt like an oddball (and who hasn't) then you can appreciate these words by Henry David Thoreau: "If a man does not keep pace with his companions, perhaps it's because he hears a different drummer. Let him step to the music he hears, however measured or far away."

All of us are stepping to some kind of music. There is a driving force in life that causes us to do what we do. Something motivates us. There is a silent beating of the drums that calls us to take certain roads in life, and at times, according to poet Robert Frost, it is "the road less traveled." Others may not be able to understand us nor agree with our actions.

Take Abraham in the Old Testament, for example. There he was on the sandy plains of Mesopotamia (1900 BCE) minding his own business, living in his comfort zone of traditions, when something began to pull at him. It wouldn't go away, and was saying, "Abram, get up off your traditions and take your people to a place that you will be shown." So, seventy-five-year-old Abram began packing while his family probably thought he was losing it. But still, he set out, not knowing where he was going. (Genesis 12:1-5)

I can see how this phenomenon has shaped my own life, though certainly not in Abrahamic proportions. When I was stationed in Newfoundland toward the end of WWII, I had a strange feeling that wouldn't go away. I talked with the base chaplain, who diagnosed it as homesickness. I was homesick alright, but the silent beating of the drums led me to the ministry, and I had no idea what was in store. This kind of thing is very common, I'm sure.

Before all of this, I had thought of pursuing law or being a chiropractor. My Dad had gone to chiropractors often and he showed me how to "adjust" him. I would straddle his back and twist his neck until something popped. It's a wonder I didn't kill the man. I'm not sure why I thought of law, except that

I had the impression they made more money than anyone. (My apologies to chiropractors and lawyers).

I've heard the silent beating of the drums many times. In 1946, I began my college career. During the first semester, I wrote a term paper entitled *The Race Problem in America (As Black Americans See It)*. I still have it. I don't write this boastfully, but it was clear to me then that things in this country HAD to change. My sensitivity to this issue may have come (in part) due to the fact that I had served in the military alongside people of many races, and some were good friends.

I have lived to see change that I never thought possible back then. Early in my ministry I was the pastor of a church where several members wanted me to resign because I had voted for the public school system to remain open. My statement to the church's administrative board went something like this: "As long as I live, I will believe that God is the Creator of all people, regardless of color or creed, and we have no right to look down on anyone." I stayed two more years.

The drums keep beating and attitudes are changing. More and more people are feeling the need to move away from old worn-out negative prejudices, realizing they are counter-productive. We are indeed living in a new day.

In Michelle Obama's biography, there is a reference to the time she spoke to USC students: "When you are on a college campus, it is a rare opportunity that you have to live with people who are not like you, who live in a different way." She added: "We are still a nation that is too divided, and we live in isolation from one another." (*Michelle: A Biography* by Liza Mundy. Simon and Schuster, 2008, pp.118-119)

So let us pray for the day to come when we no longer refer to "black" or "white" or any other color, but to look upon ALL people as children of God.

And let us give thanks that many are willing to listen to the "silent beating of the drums," moving this nation a little closer to God's Will in the 21st century. Amen

"There is no longer Greek and Jew, Barbarian, slave and free. But Christ is all and in all." (Colossians 3:11.)

God does not deliver us FROM trouble but is with us IN trouble.

WISDOM FROM A SANDBOX

It's easy to forget how to play. We can take ourselves and "the world" too seriously, and find ourselves whining, and complaining about almost everything. We can go along as serious adults so long that we forget what it means to have fun.

One of the things I've enjoyed about being in Louisiana is the "pass a good time" philosophy that prevails, even during hard times. All of us have a child within who wants to laugh and sing and dance and pass a good time. Children have a natural instinct about all of this, and they don't have any problem having fun, unless, of course, they live in a sick environment where there is fear and dread of punishment.

Jesus loved little children. "Let the little children come to me and forbid them not, for to such belongs the Kingdom of God," He said (Mark 10:14). He compared them to the Kingdom of God, which meant that we need to be childlike, playful, sincere, generous and happy.

One summer I was in Biloxi, and I heard a commotion outside my room. Two little boys were having a race with two hermit crabs. They were really caught up in it. I joined in. After the race, they tried to give me both crabs to bring home. When we were leaving, one said, "See ya next summer." Children can have fun with almost anything. A stick becomes a scepter. A stone, a throne. Two minutes later, the stick is a magic wand and the stone, a pet dragon.

Author Francis Thompson put it this way: "Do you know what it's like to be a child? It is to have a spirit yet streaming from the waters of baptism; it is to believe in love, to believe in loveliness, to believe in belief, and it is to turn pumpkins into coaches, and mice into horses, lowliness into loftiness and nothing into something, for each child has its fairy godmother in its soul."

One of my favorite books is <u>All I Really Need to Know I Learned In Kindergarten</u>. It's one of those books that I read again and again. Robert

Fulghum believes that wisdom was not found at the top of the graduate-school mountain, but in the sand pile at Sunday school.

These are some of the things he said he learned:

Share everything.
Play fair.
Put things back where you found them.
Clean up your own mess.
Don't take anything that isn't yours.
Don't hit people.
Say you're sorry when you hurt somebody.
Wash your hands before you eat.
Flush.
Warm cookies and cold milk are good for you.
Live a balanced life.
Learn some and think some and draw and paint and sing and dance
and play and work every day some.
Take a nap every afternoon
Say please and thank you.
When you go out into the world, watch out for traffic, hold hands and
stick together.

I know, of course, that not all children are angelic. Some turn out to be bullies or brats. Surveys show that the majority of these kids come from dysfunctional families and have overbearing mothers and/or fathers. Home-influence has the greatest impact on almost all of us. Seeds of trusting in God are planted in childhood.

Little Billy came running in the house, crying that Ruthie had hit him while they were playing. "You mean you let a mere girl hit you?" his father asked. The boy answered, "Dad, girls aren't as MERE as they used to be."

It's strange how quickly children grow up and leave to be on their own. In many ways it was hard letting go our three daughters and two sons when the time came. Yet, I would not keep them, even if I could have; it is their turn. They must have their own try at being responsible adults. They are not children. Maybe some of the things we tried to teach them rubbed off on their children and their children's children. We prepared them to be independent. They don't belong to us. They never did. We had custody for a little while.

They are God's children, as we all are. Hopefully, the lessons learned in a sandbox will stay with us.

> Never trust a doctor whose plants have died.

NEED A PERSONALITY
MAKE-OVER?

Referring to himself, a friend said, "God never made a better person, I just can't live up to it, that's all." Wrong. All of us can make improvements. We can begin with a positive attitude toward life. If you find yourself in complaint-city, always griping about something, you can get out by making up your mind to be more positive.

We want to be happy, useful, good, honest and upright people. So what happens when we betray our own values, and go against the very things we know to be right?

Take this true example. I officiated at a certain wedding years ago. I've never married a happier couple. Their laughter was contagious, their happiness was genuine. Then, many years after the honeymoon, they began to be bored with each other, and he began abusing his body with alcohol. She started taking anti-depressants. There was a bit of impatience here, an unkind word there. She finally said "Our marriage needs a make-over, let's get help." He said there was nothing wrong with him, and if she wanted to get help, she could. She cried almost every day. He criticizes her for little things. She points out to him that he is a rotten alcoholic. Finally, they both said they had enough and off to the lawyer and divorce court they went. It was over, leaving two sons and one daughter who had registered every domestic shock, and will be affected emotionally the rest of their life, to say nothing of two unhappy souls who had a failed relationship.

So what happens to people when they want to be good and to do the right thing but something happens, and changes their personal history? What happens when a person turns sour on the world, and nothing seems right? I think we need to examine our spiritual reservoir from time to time. We may be running on "empty." In the 12th chapter of Romans, we find these pertinent words: "Do not be conformed to this world, but be transformed by the renewal of your mind, that you may prove what is the will of God, what is good and acceptable and perfect." Yes, the mind can be renewed, and as someone has said, "The mind is the builder." As Jesus said in the third chapter of John: "You must be born anew."

Some may try to explain the above case by pointing to Satan as the adversary: "Old Satan got into both of them and destroyed their marriage." I think that's a cop-out, scape-goat thinking, as if to say that some "force" on the outside destroyed a good relationship. I don't believe that at all. I *think* it's the failure to ADMIT it when you're wrong and the LACK of determination to make changes, in attitude and behavior. It's a pride problem or ego-problem, and yes, a spiritual problem too. All of us are born with the spirit of good and evil, and we sometimes ALLOW the spirit of evil to take over. And the spirit of good doesn't seem to be strong enough to counter it, or so we think. So we go on hurting the very people we love and destroying relationships we once treasured.

Behavioral scientists tell us that our behavior is as much as 65% genetic. Unless we break the cycle out of pure determination, we act the way we do because of our mamas and papas. Oh, occasionally we may get a gene from Uncle Harry or Aunt Sally, but basically we are shaped in the womb. Yes, genetic influence is tremendous but so is our environment, and the personal choices we make. Whatever the case, we CAN be transformed.

I know a psychologist in Houston who analyzed outstanding executives for big companies across the U.S. He has taken the information that came from Plato and Hippocrates eons ago and devised a questionnaire to give him four basic personality types. (There is a negative and positive side to both.) They are: 1. Thinkers. 2. Counters. 3. Doers 4. Talkers.

1. THINKERS: They have a "better" idea. They function of the thinking level. We owe a great deal to people like Steve Job, Bill Gates, Einstein, Edison, etc.
2. COUNTERS: They live by "numbers." They have lists, charts and have a "system" for doing just about everything. Strictly left-brain, they are not happy at cocktail parties. They'd rather face the computer than people.
3. DOERS: They don't have to think about it, they just do it. If the grass needs cutting, they cut it. You don't have to be in the mood to get the job done. You just do it.
4. TALKERS: The way you solve a problem is to get together and talk about it. "This is what I hear you saying." They analyze words and say it one way and then another. They can chew on a problem for hours and never find a solution. Sometimes they just go off and leave their mouth running.

His point is this; it's easy to get stuck in one of these positions and say "that's just the way I am." And think it's too late to change. Not so. God has given us the WILL, the ability, to create our own personality type. We can change directions, learn new skills and develop new habits. We can read how others went through the dark periods of their life and how they changed directions. We can pray for a better attitude toward ourselves and life in general. The sky is the limit with "make-over" possibilities. We have to BELIEVE we can do it.

Enough preaching, time for a smile.

I was recuperating one time from major surgery and had to be out of the pulpit for several weeks, when I received a get-well card from a parishioner who scribbled these words inside the card: "Henry, I hope this will give you time to write some new sermons." IT DID!

SLOW ME DOWN, LORD

"Slow me down, Lord, I'se going too fast;
I can't see my brother when he's walking past."
(Anon)

If the Lord doesn't slow us down, the traffic cops in Woodworth or Dry Prong will be glad to do it. And for a very good reason. We're going too fast, not only on the highways but in everyday life.

One of the first things we do when we get up in the mornings is to see what time it is. And then we let time dominate us throughout the day. Hurrying has become a dangerous addiction.

Larry Dorsey, an American physician, coined the term "time-sickness" to describe the notion that time is getting away, and there's not enough of it, and we have to run just to keep up. One of the signs of this affliction is when your mind keeps racing after your body stops.

I've belonged to the "cult" of speed for a long time. There seems to be a certain virtue in saying, "I've really been busy." Carl Honore, in his book <u>In Praise of Slowness</u>, says we are driving the planet and ourselves towards burnout. He points out that we have become so "time-sick" that we neglect our families, and our friends. We are so turbocharged that we are paying a big price in many ways. We eat too much unhealthy fast food, obesity is increasing, and we're not getting enough sleep. Also, automobile accidents caused from drowsiness are too frequent. The main communication in families these days is posting notes on the fridge, or while eating in front of the TV. Many parents spend more time dealing with email than talking or playing with their kids.

Our obsession with going faster has triggered lost tempers in supermarkets, road rage, relationship rage, stress-related illnesses, increased suicide (especially among teens) and on and on.

So, I've wondered—is it possible to slow down in a world that demands that we get it done in less and less time? I believe it is, and there are many signs that point in that direction Many people are realizing that "slow can be beautiful." There's a healthy increase in gardening, knitting, cooking slowly at home, reading to children, doing yoga, painting, dancing, playing music, etc. All of this is to re-connect with ourselves and others and to live healthier and happier life-styles.

The other day, I walked to the post office, the grocery store and the bank. No big deal, yet I did see the world in a little different way and noticed things I'd overlooked while driving. And I laughed when someone offered me a ride.

People often ask me if I am learning to cook. My usual reply is, "Yes, it's called hunger." Actually it's much more than that for I'm learning to prepare food from scratch and eating out less. Also, I am doing art at my own pace without having to meet deadlines for art exhibits. I keep telling myself that time should be our slave, not our master.

I believe this is a spiritual matter, a need of the heart and the soul to go at a slower pace, and, as they say, "to smell the roses." I believe our faith in God can grow better in the soil of slowness. "Be still and know that God is God," said the Psalmist. (Psalms 46:10)

Of course, "speeding it up" can be fun and productive and needed at times. But we do need what the slow-movement offers, because it is so evident that we are over-connected technologically and under-connected personally.

The writer of Ecclesiastes (chapter 3) makes it clear that there is a season, a time for everything under heaven and that God made everything beautiful in its time.

Prayer: "Dear God, when I first wake up in the morning, help me not to look at the clock, but to be thankful that you have given me another slice of time and another season to enjoy." Amen.

Don't talk unless you can improve on silence.

THE HEALING ART OF LISTENING

One of the most important things we can do for another human being is simply to listen. This is especially true when the other person is hurting. Some of us are so anxious to "get our two cents in" that we fail to listen carefully. Many marriages suffer because the parties involved turn deaf ears to what is being said, or are so insensitive that they simply don't hear the pain.

In our society, it is common to keep our pain to ourselves. The greater the suffering, the more we withdraw. We've been taught to bear the burden privately, to get on with life, and not to be a "wimp." Also, we feel uncomfortable when others voice their pain, loss or despair. We believe that we must try to fix it, or make it go away, and that it's not enough just to listen with compassion.

Everyone has a story to tell—a story about their loss or how they were abused. Telling our stories, however painful, and being listened to, is one of the best ways to heal.

According to Margaret J. Wheatley, author of Turning to One Another, to the second generation of Holocaust survivors, the children of those who survived the death camps, the impact of silence is clear. "When parents spared their children the stories of the horror they had experienced, the children grew up depressed, sometimes suicidal. Children often know the secrets of their parents. They intuit that something important is not being shared, and cannot interpret their feelings that something is terribly wrong. So, as children do, they assume responsibility for these bad feelings. As they mature, this self-loathing is manifested as depression or even self-destruction."

When we tell our stories, or listen to others tell theirs, we listen with compassion, we don't judge, interrupt or give advice. We just enter for a moment into the other person's painful world. Being understood and heard is the prelude to much-needed healing.

One other thought: In our busy, hectic and noisy world, it is important also to listen to God. Prayer is asking; meditation is listening. I believe we need to meditate on God's Word and allow God's Spirit to lead us before we spring into action. Real power is not found in Superman or Spiderman, however entertaining that may be. None of us will ever reach the place where we can out-muscle locomotives or swing from building to building. However, we can gain inner strength through meditative listening to the "small, still voice of God." And the more we do this, the better we are at listening effectively to each other.

THE TIME OF
YOUR LIFE...IS NOW

The Williams Brothers' Store is still going strong in my home town of Philadelphia, Mississippi. Established in 1907, it hasn't seen many renovations since. But that's the magic of the place. I always feel that I am walking back in time when I go there, absorbing the sights and smells of everything from hoop cheese to cowboy boots.

Thank you, dear Lord, that there are some things in my life that remain more or less the same. There are so many times when I want everything to STAY PUT, and for time not to go so fast. And yes, the older I get, the faster it seems to go.

I must confess, Lord that I have said, "I don't have time" too often.

I'm so busy, you know. I've got to get this done while there's time. I feel hurried and anxious and I'm trying to save time. But Lord, somebody must have made a mistake somewhere, because the years come and go so quickly and life is so short, and I still have many things I want to do while there's time.

Why does it HAVE to be this way, Lord? And there's so many changes. And so many of my friends are looking old and wrinkled. I got Christmas cards from some with their family pictures. I wouldn't dare send them my picture because I don't want them to feel bad.

Dear God, does EVERYTHING have to keep changing? Just when I get used to something, there it goes again, a new challenge, and strange new doors keep opening and familiar faces disappear. What's going on?

What's that, Lord? Uh, yes, I guess I do have enough time, all the time you've given me. I have as much time as I need to fill it up to the brim. I need to see time as your gift to me, and I don't want to use it up without seeing as a precious gift. Deep down, I want to honor you with my time, and spend it as wisely as I can.

TIME says to us: "Put your life in order. Put priority on the things that last, on people you love, on ideals you dream about. Make life as wonderful and as beautiful as you can for those around you, and let the Gracious Love of God enfold you."

So the next time I go to the Williams Brothers' Store, I hope I run into old friends, and...

"Oh, excuse me, sir, I'd like a half pound of hoop cheese."

REAL ROLE MODELS

Do you remember the TV series *What's My Line*, featuring 3 people who impersonated the same person? Each posed as the same individual and after being questioned by the panel, they asked the real "John Doe, the plumber" to please stand up. It was usually the least likely person.

I thought about that show recently when I read an article by Ben Stein, columnist, and international speaker. Here's a quote from his final column.

"How can a man or woman who makes an eight figure wage and lives in insane luxury really be a star in today's world, if by "star" we mean someone bright and powerful as a role model? Real stars are not riding around in the backs of limousines or in Porsches or eating raw fruit while Vietnamese girls do their nails. They can be interesting, nice people but they are not heroes to me any longer."

Amen, Ben. And thanks for reminding me of the U.S. soldier in Bagdad, who saw a little girl playing with a piece of unexploded ordinance, pushing her aside and throwing himself on it just as it exploded. He left a family desolate in California and a little girl ALIVE in Bagdad. He's the REAL thing.

And I also thought about 70-year-old Steve Bonfanti of Baton Rouge who was badly beaten, losing 8 teeth and having to have 40 stitches in his upper lip, after slowing down in a school zone, and later stunned a judge by saying he wanted to give $41,000.00 to his attacker's young daughter.

I am reminded once again that genuine role models are not necessarily those who receive awards for acting, singing, dancing or playing ball better than anyone else, although many are doing great things with their money. In today's world, heroes are more like the men and women who patrol the streets of Baghdad, Mosul, Kabul and other places, risking their lives daily, trying to protect people from terrorists. They are also social workers, teachers, firemen, paramedics, volunteers and many others who work unselfishly to serve others.

Jesus of Nazareth once said: "Whosoever will be chief among you, let him be your servant." (Matthew20:27)

So, it seems to me that those who live and work and help others - including parents who give their children unconditional love - are the greatest among us. As someone put it, "Helping others is our main excuse for living." They are the real idols.

One of the most humbling experiences of my life came in the late nineties, when my oldest son was the keynote speaker for the New York Life Insurance International Meeting in Barcelona, Spain. In his speech, Steve said "My mother and father are in the audience this evening and they are my real heroes." The crowd gave us a standing ovation. Tears came quickly and I found myself wishing I had given more time and attention to our children when they were growing up, instead of spending so much time in church committees.

May God help us all. Amen

INTERRUPTIONS CAN BE
A BLESSING

Life is no bowl of cherries. It's full of the unwanted, and unexpected. It's full of interruptions.

Life is going along at a steady pace, and then visit to a Doctor. Then a biopsy. And then a change of schedule and an effort to change a few habits. What next? Self-pity, or a prayer for a new beginning?

George Washington's heart was set on being a sailor in the British Navy. He even had his ticket for the trip to England. At the last moment circumstances prevented his going. He was deeply disappointed. However, something better came along. Instead of becoming a sailor, Washington became the first President of the United States.

David Livingtone planned on being a missionary to China. However, the Opium War prevented him from entering China, so he turned to Africa, and found God's Will for his life.

Disappointments can become God's appointments. Interruptions can open new doors for those who are willing to risk change. Being flexible is a great asset. Sometimes the detours of life an be a blessing.

I was on vacation awhile back in a place overlooking a large lake. Early one morning, I went to a beautiful, quiet place to meditate and pray. In a few minutes, I heard a big splash close to the lake's edge. "Lord, I'll be back in a minute," I said as I put my Bible down and hurried to fetch my rod and reel. In no time at all, I met my interruption by pulling a nice bass to the bank. I wish all of my interruptions were that enjoyable and simple.

It seems to me that losing a loved one is the most difficult interruption of all. Your world is torn apart, and you wonder if you can ever make a good adjustment. Suddenly your life changes. You try to move on, develop new interests, make new friends, but still—there's a hole in your heart. Peace comes only when you realize that you can't OWN anyone, and that this person was a gift from God in the first place. Peace comes when you can accept death, not as an enemy but as part of the scheme of things. This is especially true when the deceased has lived and long, full life. Death for a young person can be a different matter altogether.

I like the story of Lin Yutang, a Chinese philosopher, who lived with his son on a farm. One day, their horse wandered away, and a friend said, "Oh, how terrible." Lin said, "How do you know it's terrible?"

A week later the horse brought a whole herd of horses back. The friend said, "Congratulations on your good luck." Lin said, "How do you know that it's good luck?"

A week later Lin's son fell off of a horse and broke his leg. The friend said, "Oh, how terrible." Lin said, "How do you know it's terrible?"

A month later, war broke out and all young men were drafted except the son with the broken leg. The friend said, "What good fortune." And Lin said...

The story goes on and on, from good to bad and back to good again. There is a simple but profound truth in this saga. No event is final. How do you KNOW that something is good or bad? All of our days are not in yet. All of our experiences haven't been experienced.

One of my favorite Bible verses comes from Paul's Letter to the Romans (8:28), "All things works together for Good for those who love God and who are called according to His purpose."

We can handle our interruptions when our faith is greater than our frustrations.

> God has not promised skies always blue,
> Nor flower-strewn pathways all our lives through.
> God has not promised sun without rain,
> Joy without sorrow, peace without pain.
> But God has promised strength for the day,
> Rest from the labor, light for the way. (Anon)

It's never too late to have a childhood, but the second one is up to you.

LOVE HAS ITS OWN LANGUAGE

I visited a friend in the hospital who had gone through an ordeal that left him with the possibility of losing his life. As we talked he told me that he felt so sorry for his wife because she had stayed with him night and day and hadn't had a good night's rest in days. I said, "Mister, you don't have to feel sorry for her, cause she was doing what she wanted to do. You couldn't keep her away." And when he was discharged from the hospital, he said he seemed to see his wife and children for the first time. It's strange how much GOOD can come out of illness. Sometimes, it opens our eyes.

But love is often like that. It transforms. It does what it has to do, no two ways about it. The Greeks had a fancy word for it, *agape*, to describe unselfish, unself-centered love. It asks nothing in return.

Paul describes Agape in his letter to the Corinthians (I Cor. 13): "Love is patient and kind. It is not jealous or boastful. It is not arrogant or rude. Love does not insist on having its own way."

The Greeks had several words for love in the New Testament. Another one was *eros* which included the erotic, sensual side of love. Both *agape* and *eros* are God-given, and are natural and necessary for the betterment and the on-going of life itself. But the thing about *eros* is that it can take over and masquerade as *agape* love. In our society, *eros* seems like a naughty child acting out and acting up in ways that are self-destructive and harmful to others. It is often love gone wild, ruthless, undisciplined and exploitive.

Yet, *eros* can be beautiful. The Song of Solomon in the Old Testament describes the best side of *eros*. Listen to this: "Behold, you are beautiful, my love, your eyes are like doves behind the veil, your hair is like a flock of goats moving down the slopes of Giliad, your teeth are like a flock of shorn eyes that have come up from the washing...Upon my bed at night I sought him who my soul loves...You have ravished my heart my bride, you have ravished my heart with a glance of your eyes; how sweet is your love." (Selected verses from the Song of Solomon.)

The two basic emotional needs of human beings are to love and to be loved. Some know how to BE loved but don't know HOW to love another person. We are born selfish and some never get over it.

Having counseled married couple for decades, I have seen sex masquerading as love many times. It is conditional and says "I will love you as long as you please me." A person may not actually say this, but it's there nevertheless. *Eros* needs *agape* to rescue it from pure narcissism. A narcissist is preoccupied with him or herself to the exclusion of everyone else. They expoit others to satisfy their own need.

But back to *agape* love, the highest level of human emotion. It's the opposite of using another person to get what you want. This kind of life is responsible and generous, and sometimes, extravagant.

Look at the story in Mark's Gospel (13:1-9) about when a woman came to see Jesus when he was in Bethany. She went with a bottle of very expensive perfume to anoint Jesus for burial. Those guys sitting around were upset and asked why the perfume wasn't sold and given to the poor. Jesus told them that they would always have the poor but to leave her alone because she had done a beautiful and unselfish thing.

So we can give thanks for love when it expresses itself in wonderful and life-producing ways. Paul said this kind of love never fails.

I close with the following words that I wrote for a family wedding:

What does it mean to say, "I love you?"

In our society, to say "I love you" could mean almost anything. But within the context of Judeo-Christian values, it means, "I accept you as you are. I look upon you as a separate identity and you will always remain a person in your own right."

It means that I will not seek to change you. I will simply enjoy that which already is, and I will anticipate with joy all that CAN be as we grow and change together. Above all else, it means that I will care for you as I care for no other, without condition, except to have the privilege of returning your love and allowing you to bring out the best within me.

What does it mean to say "I love you?" It means I will care about you unselfishly as long as we live, and if God permits, I will continue to love you eternally. Amen.

We need seven hugs a day just to maintain our emotional balance.

THE ART OF BEING WRONG

The other day, I heard a preacher say that all of us are sinners and have fallen short of the glory of God. He echoed the words of Paul's letter to the Romans (3:23). If that's true (and it probably is) then we might as well do it right. In other words, we have a right to be wrong.

Before you start praying for me, let me explain. One of the greatest needs that most of us have is to be "right," no matter what. And sometimes, we go to a lot of trouble to prove it. To be wrong is a big blow to the ego.

Whoever said, "I'd rather be RIGHT than to be the President," never got to be President.

Having done a little marriage counseling through the years, I can honestly say that many people would rather be "right" than to be married. Or to have friends. Or to have a close family.

So where did this tremendous urge come from? Most of us have been carefully taught to do the right thing in our homes, churches, and schools. We are rewarded if we do it right and we might be punished if we do it wrong.

Here is a 12-year-old child who has been playing the piano since the age 7. She has learned half notes, whole notes, octaves, keeping time and so on. She is applauded for playing it right, which is the way it ought to be, of course.

Or here is a kid who goes out for football. He's taught how to block, tackle, intercept a pass, and run like crazy. Dad gets really excited about that and yells at the top of his lungs when he makes a touchdown, "That's MY boy." He did it right.

Maybe somewhere along the way we need to teach our kids the art of being "wrong." We need to know how to swallow our pride, and to be smart enough to cut the other person a little slack for the sake of a good relationship. Many people carry grudges because they have an "I know I'm right" hang up.

My point is this: Being "right" is not enough. It's the attitude toward our rightness that's important. We can be self-righteous, arrogant and rigid.

I know a family who is divided over their inheritance. Half of them aren't speaking to the other half. Both sides say they are right. The family remains split.

I was a guest at a dinner party one time. The host couple had gone to Lafayette a few days before. The conversation went something like this:

Wife: "We went to Lafayette last Thursday."
Husband: "No honey, it was Wednesday."
Wife: "Well anyway, we ran into Bob and Lindy."
Husband: "No baby, we saw them in Baton Rouge. We saw Gus and Judy in Lafayette."

About this time, the atmosphere changes.

Wife: (with tight lips) "Well, why don't you tell them about it, MR. RIGHT?" Then, there was this unmistakable we-will-deal-with-this-later look.

Why will some of us do anything to carry a point? Why do we have to be right? It's called "control," among other things. The human ego has a feast over this issue. What seems to be right may turn out to be wrong and what seems to be wrong may turn out to be right.

Jesus told a parable about a Pharisee and a tax collector who went into the temple to pray (Luke 18:9-14). The Pharisee, who had kept all the rules, said, "God, I'm thankful I'm not like other people, thieves, rogues, adulterers, or even like this tax collector. I fast twice a week and I give a tenth of all my income," But the tax collector wouldn't even look up at Heaven, but was beating his breast and saying, "God, be merciful to me, a sinner." Then Jesus said, "I tell you, this man went down to his home justified rather than the other, for all who exalt themselves will be humbled but all who humble themselves will be exalted."

Now, that's the art of being wrong. The tax collector didn't brag about anything or hide from the facts. He simply said that he was wrong, and he said it with humility.

When you stop and think about it, this sort of thing happens between nations. Wars exist because "we are right and others are wrong."

I saw a road-side sign that said "Get Right With God." How do we know we've covered all of our bases? We don't. That's why we lean on the forgiving Grace of God. "Amazing Grace, how sweet the sound, that saved a wretch like me. I once was lost but now am found, was blind but now I see."

LET THE RIVER TAKE YOU

I went tubing one time along the Tangipahoa River with a friend from the La. Dept. of Tourism and Recreation. His assignment was to take pictures as we floated by the beauties of nature. At the beginning of our expedition, he realized that I was a little nervous about being in such a small tube and the prospects of turbulence in the river.

"You will enjoy it," he assured me, "Just relax and let the river take you."

"THAT'S what I'm afraid of," I laughed half-heartedly.

"Let the river take you." These words lodged in the back of mind as an analogy of life itself. I can see the wisdom of relaxing and letting life happen as it will, and does—despite our efforts to alter its course. Life keeps moving, and changing whether we are willing to go along with the ride or not. We can try to control, possess, manipulate, yell and scream, but the river keep flowing right along.

One of the Greek Philosophers, Epictetus, said, "We never step into the same river twice." Change is inevitable. Unhappiness results when we fail to deal constructively with what IS, rather than what OUGHT to be.

Example: We can resent getting older, losing our energy, finding more wrinkles, experiencing more and more losses, but the facts still remain. We can butt our heads against reality but reality holds. Many times I'd like to change reality, especially when it come to the loss of loved ones. But instead of asking WHY did this happen, I need to ask HOW can I deal with it?

Easterners tell us that suffering is caused by "desire," insisting that we find personal fulfillment "MY WAY," and when this doesn't happen, we can become depressed or addicted to destructive habits. The egoistic mind can rule our lives to the point that we can become enslaved to wanting what we want when we want it. The egoistic mind can give us a lot of "shoulds" and "oughts," and create for us a very stressful life if it doesn't happen the way we want it.

In the Sermon on the Mount, Jesus speaks, "Which of you by being anxious can add one cubit to his life?" He goes on to say, "O Ye of little faith." (Matthew 6)

Faith. Letting go. Yielding to the flow of life. Trusting God during all of the stages of life. It is changing what we can but not resenting nor resisting inevitable change. I believe this is what Jesus was talking about. Let the river take you. Trust tomorrow.

By ourselves, we can become adrift in a huge sea of water without an anchor. But our trust in God helps us to see that we are not left with our own devices to survive. The Psalmist reassures us: "He leads me beside still waters, he restores my soul" (Psalm 23)

DON'T ROCK THE BOAT

When I read the story in the 4th chapter of The Gospel of Mark where Jesus is on the boat with His Disciples as the storm approaches, I think of that old saying, "Don't rock the boat." It seems that this is what the Disciples were doing. They panicked, thinking they were about to drown. There are times when fear visits all of us. It's easier to say, "Don't be afraid, don't worry," than it is not to be afraid, or to worry.

We will probably never see the day when we will be entirely free from some kind of anxiety or frustration. As long as we have children, or loved ones who are ill, or live in the path or hurricanes and earthquakes and so forth, we will experience fear and frustration. If I know anything about God's Will, it is that we find peace of mind even in the midst of the storm. Our faith is not simply a problem-centered faith, nor is it an insurance policy against problems. But it is our main source of help and hope. Our faith sustains us in the good times, in all the joys of life and brighter days.

Having said this, let me give you three don'ts before you throw in the towel.

1. **Don't Stuff Your Fears on the Inside—Let Them Out**. Ventilate your feelings with someone you can trust. As psychologist William James put it, "All of us need to exteriorize our rottenness." I heard a psychiatrist say that there is something wrong with all of us, every single one of us. All of us are neurotic about something. It depends upon the degree. If we don't recognize this fact, we are kidding ourselves. The problems of the world do not point to political structures of societal breakdowns, but to the individual—imperfect people, struggling toward wholeness and health.

    A friend gave me a book by George Best, who wrote, "Go ahead and cry; please don't hold back because of me. Your tears will cleanse your soul, allowing you to release those emotions inside. Big boys do cry and so do big girls." Remember that old song, "Pack up your troubles in your old kit bag and smile, smile, smile." Well, that's just about the worst thing one can do. We don't deal with problems by simply packing them away.

2. **Don't Give in to Your Moods**. Patience is a wonderful virtue, especially in coping with moods, because sooner or later, they pass or change. The human spirit operates in cycles. Couples who have been married any length of time know about their spouse's moods. They know when it is wise to say something or not to say something. Back when I was a Pastor, Mondays usually found me at my lowest ebb. I told parishioners that if they must call me on Monday mornings, please be sweet and kind. But by Tuesday, I was usually "up" again.

One of the great values of quiet meditation is that it helps me to reclaim my center: It restores my soul. I can't say enough about the importance of meditation. Fifteen or twenty minutes of quiet contemplation daily is necessary for good spiritual health.

3. **Don't Let the Storms of Life Blow You in Different Directions**. Everyone needs a cause, a purpose or a goal that is worth getting out of bed for. Some people are pushed around by their problems, rather than being led by their dreams. A friend said to me recently, "I feel that my life is on hold. I don't know what I'm here for." An empty life can lead to much boredom, loneliness and depression. We need something to fight for, believe in and work toward.

One day Jesus was on the water with His Disciples, and when the storm came up, His Disciples were terribly afraid. They asked Jesus if He cared whether they drowned or not. Jesus, not being blind to their danger, told them, "Peace, be still." Was He speaking to the storm or to His Disciples? I believe He was saying to these nervous, distraught people: Why are you afraid? Where is your faith? Peace, be still. Don't you know that God is never defeated? Don't you know that even the bottom of the sea is the hollow of His hand?"

However good or bad a situation is, just remember: This too shall pass.

BEATITUDES FOR FATHERS
AND OTHER IMPERFECT PEOPLE

Blessed are fathers and other imperfect people who are doing the best they can do to fulfill their role. Of course, the male species isn't always clear about what is expected. We don't always know whether to be macho or mild, passive or aggressive, dominant or servile. John Eldredge, in his book Wild at Heart, says we are so tame that we are somewhat unchallenged, and too domesticated. He said men need three things: A battle to fight, an adventure to live, and a beauty to rescue. (Sounds like men from a tribe.)

Blessed are those who can balance their work and relationships. I know a young man who was having a "wild" time holding a night job, attending day classes, supporting a wife and two children. I asked him how could he balance all of it, and he said being a father was by far the most challenging job of all, but he was determined to get his degree. His wife said she was challenged with "patience." It's all about relationships. You can have all of the academic degrees in the world and fail to nurture good relationships.

Blessed are those who are patient. The world might be changing but patience will never go out of style. It is said that women are more patient than men, generally speaking. They are probably correct. I know I pray for patience as much as anything else.

Blessed are those who can control their tongue, who are more complementary and less critical. Paul wrote in Ephesians 6:4, "Fathers, don't provoke your children to anger, but bring them up in the discipline and instruction of the Lord." Blessed are those who make peace with spilled milk, muddy shoes and loud noises.

Blessed are those who can restrain their temper when Junior's bedroom looks like a tornado hit it. "Because I said so," is not a wise response to anything.

I know a couple who said they try to honor the Biblical advice to not let the sun go down when they are angry. She said there are many "late sunsets." Blessed are those who are careful to be "on time." I had an outdoor wedding one time. It was supposed to start at seven p.m. Seven came, no groom. Seven thirty, no groom. Eight o'clock and no groom. About 8:15, the groom showed up. By this time, the bride was livid, her mascara had run, her patience had run out. We proceeded with the tense ceremony and at the close, the groom leaned over and whispered to me, "Pray for me tonight." Strange request.

Blessed are fathers who take a leadership role in the home, especially in matters of faith. They honor the Ten Commandments as well as other Biblical teachings. The Apostle Paul had some good advice for couples when he said, "Be subject to each other out of reverence for Christ. Husbands, love your wives as your own body…" (Eph. 6:21) For an old bachelor in a male dominated society, Paul did okay.

Blessed are you for reading this and saying, "I'll do it"

Blessed are couples who can nurture each other long after their honeymoon.

If I should ask you to name the 2006 winner of the Nobel Peace Prize, or the winner of the 2005 Super Bowl, or who was crowned Miss America in 2008, you may have a few blank moments. But if I should ask you who encourages you most in life, and who has loved you unconditionally, and who has graced your life with forgiving love, you could name them without blinking an eye, because they are written in your heart.

Blessed are those who teach their kids social graces and people skills, such as looking into the eyes of a person when talking, or offering a firm handshake or saying please or thank you. Also, praise be to fathers who teach their teenagers "highway manners," the safety of driving without a cell phone glued to their ear. This may save their life.

A FAITH WORTH HAVING

Psalm 121 offers us a faith worth having by reminding us that our horizon needs to expand. We can be so wrapped up in our personal world that we may never get beyond the skyline of self-centered concerns. The Psalmist said: "I will lift up my eyes unto the hill." When the Hebrew were exiles in Babylon, there were no hills. It was an alien land. Babylon was the business and commercial center of the ancient world. Its great buildings reflected the achievements of humanity. They longed for the hills of home.

Today, we can be so blinded by technological advancements that we may feel that we are in charge or in control of life itself. Then, when our world falls apart through a personal loss, we are left stranded with ourselves. We have nowhere to turn unless we look to God for strength and guidance.

I recommend Fr. Richard Rohr's book Job and the Mystery of Suffering. He says, "Most of us are terribly upset that we are not God. It ticks us off that another is in charge and we aren't." I believe he has a point. I have often thought, "Now, if I were God, I wouldn't let good people suffer, and I would change this or that, etc." I would like to be able to "fix it" and to be in control. I suspect that there are many others who feel the same way. But when we realize that God is God, and we are His creatures, we think in a different way. And when we realize that God is not out to "zap" it to us, we are really making progress towards the truth.

Rohr goes on to point out that we have misunderstood God's justice system. God is not an eternal torturer or punisher. He says that Sheol is a non-world, a denial of all that we know here. The Greeks had the concept of Hades, which eventually developed into what Christians think of as Hell—a place of everlasting punishment. The New Testament metaphor of "Gehenna" (commonly known as Hell), refers to the garbage dump outside Jerusalem, "where the worm never dies and the fire never goes out." (Isaiah 60:24). Perhaps we have overdeveloped a system of eternal punishment, and underdeveloped a system of God's unconditional love and forgiving Grace. It's a Grace that can save a sinner like me.

If we miss the meaning of "For God so loved the world," then we have a distorted view of the nature of God, and a faith that never looks beyond ourselves. God redeems us from the temptations and troubles of this world. With that kind of faith, all else falls into place:

"I will lift up my eyes to the hills,
From where does my help come?
My help comes from the Lord,
Who made Heaven and earth." (Psalm 121)

WHEN GOD COMES INTO FOCUS

The 42nd Psalm is a very special one for me:

"As a deer longs for flowing streams,
So my soul longs for you, O God,
My soul thirsts for God,
For the Living God.
When shall I come and behold the face of God?"

This phrase, "the Face of God," interests me to the point of asking: When have I seen the Face of God? I could name many ways that God has come into focus for me, but let me mention only a few here.

First, when I look into the face of a newborn baby, I feel God's Presence. Here is the miracle and mystery of creation, all wrapped up in blue or pink, and I always go to the level of awe and wonder. Someone has said that a baby is God's opinion that the world should go on.

Then, God comes into focus for me when I see families who love each other; who trust each other; who forgive each other. I also find God's face in the beauty of the world around me. Jesus called our attention to the "birds of the air" and "the lilies of the field." When I hear the frogs along the bayou, or watch a mother bird feed her little ones, or see the giant oak trees with their sideburns of moss, God comes into focus in a real way.

I must mention also that God comes into focus for me during the dark night of the soul. Most of the time, this happens in retrospect—after the fact. I can look back on difficult situations and realize that God was there before I was. Jesus gave us only one sign, which was the sign of Jonah. This means that we must go into the belly of a whale, into the darkness and hopelessness before we can be spit out on the shores of change and renewal. Then we can say, "He restoreth my soul."

The Psalmist also said, "My tears have been my food day and night." We can be thankful for the gift of tears, for they help us to wash "it" out. If we couldn't cry, we would be in real trouble! Perhaps violent.

God comes into focus in a variety of ways, but surely when I feel God's love and grace. Christianity is not about dogma, doctrine or denominations. It is longing for God "as the deer longs for the flowing streams." Amen.

THE MOST IMPORTANT WORD

Several newspaper editors decided to find the most important and expressive word in the English language, as well as other emotion-packed words. They conducted a survey, and the results were not very surprising. They found that the bitterest word was ALONE. The most cruel word was REVENGE. The saddest word was FORGOTTEN. The most revered word was MOTHER. And the most important and beautiful word in the English language was LOVE.

Of course, there many definitions and levels of love, but I will refer to the highest expression of unselfish, non-egotistical and self-giving type.

I remember a debate we had in high school. The question was: Is it better to have loved and lost than to never have loved at all? I don't remember what I said but I do remember taking the affirmative, for I believe that true love is never lost. We become better people by doing so, although there is risk involved.

C. S. Lewis puts it well: "To love at all is to be vulnerable. Love anything and your heart will certainly be wrung and possibly be broken. If you want to make sure of keeping it intact, you must give your heart to no one, not even an animal."

So, some never take this risk and become bitter, cynical and isolated from relationships as much as they can. And their life is usually empty, cold and very lonely.

Loving God is a little like falling in love. Somehow the world looks a little different. You are no longer bound by ego, and you discover that love is actually a verb. It is something you DO rather than something you merely feel. You begin to find God not only in the beauty around you, but in the people who know how to love. You no longer think in terms of being a Methodist, Baptist, Catholic, Jew or Muslim. You are no longer hemmed in by labels or stereotypes or religious prejudice. You see people as children of God and you treat others like you want to be treated.

The New Testament tells us that God loves us so much that God sent Jesus of Nazareth to show us HOW it is done effectively. Jesus demonstrated this with words and deeds and kindnesses during his 3-year ministry. He was not a famous scholar, never wrote a book, and preached only one sermon that we know about. But he spent his entire life loving people (and not SCARING them) into the Kingdom of God.

When Boulder Dam was being built, 89 people lost their lives. There's an inscription there with the names of those who made the ultimate sacrifice. It reads: "Here are those who died that the desert might bloom."

Let us live a life that "blooms" in all the desert and dark places in this world.

WHEN YOUR FAITH IS TESTED

In the book of James (New Testament) we find these words: "Blessed is anyone who endures temptation, for such a one has stood the test and will receive the crown of life the Lord has promised to those who love Him." (James 11-12)

Life has a way of marching in front of us and asking, "What are you made of?" "What do you really believe in?" "How are you coping with the trials of life?" Nobody could answer those question better then Abraham (Old Testament). He was a man of faith. He had strong convictions and endured a great deal. He went out not knowing where the Lord was leading him. He dreamed of a place he would never see. He waited twenty-five years for a son. Then Isaac was born. The Bible said that God tested Abraham. In Genesis 22, we read, "I want you to take your son, Isaac, and offer him as a sacrifice on Mt. Moriah."

You can imagine how shocked Abraham was. It sounded so unreasonable, so unfair. Pagans offer human sacrifices, but not people of God. Maybe he misunderstood. Besides, God had promised to bless the nations through Isaac. How could he, if Isaac were killed?

Anyone who is close to their sons or daughters can identify with Abraham's feelings. To sacrifice one would be unthinkable. But God asked Abraham to do just that, and Abraham made preparations to obey. The next morning, he took two of his servants and left for Mt. Moriah. When they came to the foot of the mountain, Abraham told them to wait while he continued on further to worship.

When we think of worship, we think of singing and praying and reading sacred writings. But worship, according to this story, is making an offering to God. Worship is when we give up something of value for that in which we believe. It happens when we realize that God is worthy of our full loyalty and devotion. Worship, at its best, is not when we give burnt offerings or pledges, important as that may be, but it is the giving of ourselves, our willingness to serve.

Upon reaching the top of the mountain, Abraham raised his knife to kill Isaac. Then, the angel of the Lord said to him, "Abraham, Abraham, don't do that. You have proven that God is first in your life." Abraham then saw a ram caught in the bush and he grabbed it, making it a sacrificial offering instead of his son Isaac. Can you imagine how happy they were as they came down from the mountain? They must have been singing, clapping their hands and jumping up and down. Abraham stood the test.

Now, none of us will likely be called upon to sacrifice one of our children, but our faith is constantly being tested in other ways. It may be tested in our health and security. Sooner or later all of us face illness, pain, again and death of the body. And the only thing we have is our faith. Life proves to us over and over that this is not "our show," and that we are not in control.

Our faith may also be tested in our relationships. I recently attended a golden wedding anniversary. I thought: Anyone can have a big wedding and pull out all the stops, including a brass band, but it takes special people who can live together for fifty years or more. That deserves a lot of praise because it is a test of love, patience, forgiveness and faithfulness.

One other thought. We are tested in our convictions and beliefs. There was an article in the paper recently about Tom Shumake, a coach from Florence, Arizona. Tom resigned because he received a memo from the "higher ups" forbidding him to have prayer with his ball team. He said, "I had a choice, for I've prayed twenty years before and after each game with my ball team." They had won the State Championship the year previously. Tom continued, "I've tried to teach my kids to stand up to what they believe and I have to do the same." Some called him a fanatic. Others said he was a man of God. The fact speaks for itself.

We are not tested so that we can earn our salvation. That's a free gift and all we have to do is accept it. We are not tested to prove our love for God. God knows what is in our hearts already. It seems to me that we are tested so that our faith can be strengthened. When you are going through the valley of the shadow of death, it brings out the best or the worst in us. God helps us to stand every test that comes our way, and to be faithful witnesses as long as we live. Amen.

You have a right to be wrong. Smart people will admit it.

ARE YOU STRUGGLING
WITH YOUR FAITH?

A college student presented her case to me recently: "I was brought up in the church and accepted everything I heard in Sunday school and my home, and never questioned my beliefs. Then, in college, I made friends with a Muslim student and began having serious doubts about my faith. I stopped attending church on a regular basis, and I am still struggling. I don't know WHAT to believe anymore."

Can you identify with her? Some people doubt and never regain their personal beliefs. They conclude that there is nothing to all those Biblical miracles and they settle for the atheistic position, and think of God as some sort of a theological Santa Claus.

I saw this clearly when in Seminary. As a matter of fact, I went through the "doubting phase" myself. Late night discussions with classmates and patient professors helped me pursue the truth about God and to appreciate the value of diversity.

My faith, although altered many times through the years, is stronger now in some ways than ever. It is far more ecumenical, universal and inclusive. It is a far cry from the stranglehold of fundamentalism, which has always had a "smothering" effect upon me.

The words from the Psalmist, "My ways are not your ways, and my thoughts are not your thoughts," gave me permission not to understand everything and to feel okay about my limitations. But I understand enough to not believe that God is a "fix all," a kind of cosmic nursemaid, and that praying offers no guarantees against trouble. There is far too much hocus-pocus in RELIGION.

I believe also that our spiritual evolution is just beginning. Our biological evolution seems almost complete. Our spiritual evolution is unfolding. That is, we are beginning to face the issues that divide humanity: race, class, nationality, blood, religion, etc. We are beginning to see what it means to relate to those who are different. And I believe this is what FAITH is all about. Jesus of Nazareth did not intend to begin a NEW world religion. He wanted people to love God and to love each other, as well as to love themselves. In other words, relationships are those things that really matter. Religion can and does get in the way, especially when people worship the Bible instead of the God of all creation.

It takes a lot of denial to be an atheist. We have to work hard at NOT believing. Life itself is a great miracle. When you consider that the earth is tilted at a 23.5 degree angle and because of this we have night and day, land and sea, winter and summer, seedtime and harvest, plants and animals, rain and sunshine—when you consider this phenomenon, you MUST believe there is a Creative Mind behind creation.

When I worked in a private psychiatric hospital, a 40 year old woman in my group said she believed God kept her from doing some terrible things. One day she handed me this poem she had scribbled:

God's love for me is divine,
He cares for me all the time.
Though I have sinned and gone astray,
God walks with me all the way.
I asked God to forgive my sin,
God said, "Daughter I have already looked within,
For you are one of my angels on earth,
And I am preparing you to find your worth."

So if you are struggling with you're faith, that's okay. Maybe, just maybe, your doubts and questions will help you to find a greater relationship with God.

> It's okay to let your children see you cry. It's better than crying alone.

EVERYONE NEEDS
A LITTLE HELP

Human nature is a strange thing. All of us need a little help from time to time, as we deal with loss, grief, guilt and a few other unwantables. And yet, those who need help the most seem to want it the least. There seems to be a built-in resistance in human nature that keeps us from admitting the need for counseling, prayers or a helping hand. We can be victims of our own ego and pride. "I can take care of myself!" is a familiar refrain. But in a world like ours, it's difficult to fight battles alone.

Is this a new problem? Not at all. We still have our modem day Pharisees, who were a religious group during Biblical times that acted like they had it made. They prayed long prayers, tithed their income and fasted regularly to impress people with their superiority. It is doubtful they would listen to anybody.

Often times, religion can stand in the way of Christianity. It's easy to "get religion," to pay lip service to God by going through the motions of worship on the Sabbath without actually feeling much of anything. Even when the sermon steps on our toes, and we say, "Ouch," it seems to make very little difference in our lives.

Some people, like the rich young ruler, went to Jesus of Nazareth looking for a quick fix. He wanted Jesus to promise him eternal life immediately. When Jesus told him what he needed to do, such as getting rid of things in his life, he went away sad and disappointed. He probably thought, "I've come seeking eternal life and he talks about a give-away program?" We can put our trust in material things and lose all perspective. The young man needed to get his priorities straight, and so do we.

So, all of us would be a little better if we could accept a little help from time to time., We can start by listening to those we trust, as they try to reach out to us. Self-awareness is necessary for spiritual growth.

A friend asked me if I believed in the second coming of Christ. My answer was simple: "I don't think we've done enough about the first coming yet." Who can say that we have done enough praying, forgiving and loving? Have we taken his teachings seriously enough to say we have arrived?

I remember an evangelist who came to our church when I was a teenager. He said, "If you should die tonight, are you ready to meet God?" A much better question to me is, "If you should wake up in the morning, are you ready to live for Him?" Amen.

PEAK EXPERIENCES

Some things in life cannot be reduced to words. There are PEAK moments when the world seems to stand still, and you simply can't find enough letters in the alphabet to explain them.

It may happen during an exotic trip, a weekend retreat, your wedding day, when your children were born, during a worship service, during the Christmas season or in a number of awesome ways.

Abraham Maslow, the great psychologist, said there are peakers and non-peakers. I suppose most of us experience a combination of both. We simply cannot have peak experiences all the time. Much of life is lived on the surface—eating, sleeping, working, raising a family and plodding along in a routine way. As Shakespeare said in Macbeth, "Tomorrow and tomorrow and tomorrow, creeps in this petty place from day to day." The poet Edna St. Vincent Millay must have been really bored when she wrote, "Life goes on forever, like the gnawing of a mouse. There is this little street and this little house." Sounds like a non-peaker to me.

But, thank goodness, there are "high" moments when we are lifted above the "everydayness" of life. Great music, art, poetry, and the beauty of the world around us can put me on the top of the mountain in a heart-beat. I was in Colorado one time, driving from Denver to Aspen, and as I topped a hill, there was a beautiful panorama in front of me and I was so moved, I started singing (if you call it that): "O beautiful for spacious skies, for amber waves of grain, for purple mountain majesties above the fruited plains. America, America, God shed His Grace on thee," and so on. I don't have to be in Colorado for this to happen; I can sit on my back porch and watch the wood ducks and egrets as they sail along the bayou, and feel blessed beyond words.

Despite the negative things about our country, America is still a great idea. There's so much across this country that boggles the mind and feeds the spirit.

This is a great place to be. "America, America, God shed His grace on thee, and crown thy good with brotherhood, from sea to shining sea."

I have so many peak experiences in my memory bank. If you can look at a newborn baby, whether it's yours or not, and not experience God's miracle of creation, then something is wrong. Bad wrong. If you are willing to love and to be loved by that special person in your life, then you know that this is the stuff life is made of.

The Scriptures are packed full of those who had mountain-top experiences. The prophet Isaiah was in the Temple when he exclaimed, "I saw the Lord sitting on a throne, high and lifted up, and His robe filled the Temple." (Is. 6:1) The Psalmist David said, "O Lord, our Lord, how excellent is Your name in all the earth. You have set your glory above the Heavens." (Psalm 8:1)

Or, who can explain the unique moment when Moses encountered the burning bush? He heard a voice that said, "Take off your shoes, for you are standing on Holy Ground." He looked down and probably thought, "Looks like plain old dirt to me." And for a while, it seemed that he was going to miss the whole thing, especially when God asked him to lead the people of Israel out of Egyptian bondage. He felt unworthy and unqualified and try to get out of it by say that he was slow of speech and just couldn't pull it off. But he finally accepted the challenge and changed the course of history. (Exod. 3:1-5)

Sometimes we feel uncomfortable with peak experiences, as if we don't deserve them. Someone may say, "I think you are so wonderful," and we are thinking, "If you only knew me." It's hard for some to accept compliments, gifts or praise, and they feel awkward and clumsy. Someone comes up to you and says, "That is such a beautiful outfit, and you look so good in it." And you nervously reply, "Oh, this old thing? I've had it for years."

You are a child of God and you deserve the best. You can enjoy the peak experiences when they come, sometimes in a sudden, surprising way. Be ready for them, EXPECT them, MAKE them happen for yourself or someone else. You can lift yourself out of the hard and harsh realities of life, even for a moment, and reach for the highest mountain you can imagine.

May you enjoy many peak experiences during your time on earth.

And you know what? I truly believe this is God's Will. Amen.

Until further notice, celebrate everything.

WHO STOLE MY BUGGY?

I was in Kroger's the other day and after I yanked a grocery cart from the hungry jaws of buggy-land, I rolled it to the aisle, turned around to pick up a can of coffee, turned back around and discovered a strange woman standing next to my buggy with her purse in it. "Oh" I stammered, "Uh, I just rolled that buggy in here—it's my buggy." Her response: "No, can't you see my purse in it, so it's mine." It took me awhile, but I finally thought: "Well, if I put my wallet in your car, would that make it MY car?" But by that time, she was hurrying away with MY buggy.

Suddenly I felt like a victim. There I stood with my can of coffee and nothing to put it in. I could feel my blood pressure rising. Something came over me that was not admirable. I felt like the old Quaker when a car came by and splashed him with water, bowed his head and prayed; "May your soul rest in Heaven, and the sooner the better." Well, that evening I had a headache that would put all headaches to shame.

I realized again that anger can eat you up, giving you all kind of aches. It took me a couple of days before I could laugh about it and realize that I was truly sweating the small stuff. Also, I missed a great opportunity to say to her, "Oh, you want this buggy? Here, let me push it for you." Yeah, right. But seriously, I did miss the chance to smile and to say, "You can have it, I'll go out and get another one." Case dismissed.

Anger is a natural human emotion and is God's way of empowering us to protect ourselves and others from harm. So the problem isn't anger, it's what we do with it that matters. Uncontrolled anger can be lethal. Even if you have all the talent and money in the world, a short fuse and a hot temper can turn you into somebody that nobody wants to be around. And the sad thing about it that many people don't understand how their anger can affect their marriage, friendships, and working relationships, as well as their own health.

Uncontrolled anger can also corrupt corporations, governments and even start wars. It can be an emotional addiction that wreaks havoc everywhere it turns. Many use their cars as weapons on the highways to express their impatience and resentments, thus causing deadly accidents. Road rage is much too common.

You are the only person who can control your temper. If you've had an abusive childhood, please get professional help before you hurt your own kids, and begin a cycle of abuse. Parents create memories for their children and adults can store unhealed memories of earlier experience that need to be healed.

Happiness is a natural state of mind, but how many people go through life feeling miserable because they haven't learned how to hold their tongue or heal their wounds?

"A soft answer turns away wrath; but a harsh word stirs up anger," wrote the author of Proverbs (15:1). A good word for married couples as well as for the rest of us is, "Don't let the sun go down on your anger." (Ephesians 4:26) And here's a book I recommend: *Let the Tiger out, but Keep It on a Leash*, by Mary Ellen Halloran.

This final word: Uncontrolled anger is a spiritual problem, an UNHOLY spirit, if you please. Worst of all, it can take over the body, mind and spirit and can put a barrier between you and God.

So from now on, if someone tries to steal my buggy at Kroger's, I'll forgive them on the spot. Amen.

BEYOND THE BLUES

Feeling blue is a universal experience. Most of us have been there and done that. It's easy to feel "down" in a world where the daily news is usually negative.

Sometimes the blues turn into feelings of depression. Whether this comes from a chemical imbalance or from a life-situation, it is still depression. Feelings of hopelessness and helplessness abound.

There is an ebb and flow of stress and tension in all of life. Life without any stress would be flat and boring. But too much change too soon can leave us breathless and bewildered.

There are no magic keys to learning to cope creatively with life's difficulties, but let me make a few suggestions.

First, it is helpful to voice our feelings. Unless we can express our innermost feelings to someone, whether a counselor or a trusted friend, our feelings could get out of control.

Thousands commit suicide each year. It is believed that many of these do not really want to die. Rather, they are calling out for help. It is like saying, "Will someone please listen to me? I can't go on like this."

Seeing a competent therapist or counselor could be the answer to your need. They could help you to get to the root of your depression. Or you may need an anti-depressant to help you cope. Hope may return even as you begin to reach out for it—not by denying the situation, but by knowing that even in the pain of today, there is tomorrow. And when you realize that you are not alone, you may gain a fresh awareness of God's Presence.

In a movement from hopelessness to hope, you may have to start making decisions and different choices about life. God gives us the ability to find the help we need.

I find comfort in these words from Victor Hugo:

"Be like the bird, that pausing in her flight
On bough too slight,
Feels it give way beneath her—
Yet sings, knowing she has wings."

WORRIED SICK
AND SICK OF WORRYING

A woman came into my office one day said, "I'm worried sick and sick of worrying." Then she added, "I think the only thing that's holding me together is my hair spray."

I like to think that I am "concerned," rather than worried. I think there's a fine line between the two. When Jesus said, "Let NOT your hearts be troubled," he was not saying that we should be unconcerned. As a matter of fact, His message has always been a disturbing presence to those who are not concerned about the things that really matter in life. All of us need to be concerned about many of the issues facing our nation at this time, as well as war, crime, child abuse, poverty, drugs and so on. Many are worried about "Health Care" in this nation as if worry or anger will solve it.

There's an old saying that if you worry about what may happen and it doesn't happen, you worry in vain. And if it does happen, you worry again. So you worry twice. And it still doesn't solve anything. It takes energy to worry. We talk so much and DO so little.

When we are anxious and troubled about things that we can't control or things that have happened in the past, or the bad things we imagine about the future—it means that we are worrying foolishly. This can make us sick physically as well as emotionally.

That kind of worry is suffering in advance. It is a form of disbelief. It's a way of saying, "I can't trust God anymore; I've got to be in charge, and make it come out to suit me." It's really hard to have faith and to worry and the same time. Someone said that worrying is "practical atheism." Foolish worry is ripping God from His Sovereignty, and supposing that we must hold the world together ourselves. We need to realize that this is still God's world.

Also we need to sort through our priorities. What's really important to you? Some seem to be more concerned about making money or losing money than anything else. Do you remember the play *Death of a Salesman*? After Willie Loman took his life, his wife visited his grave one day and as she glanced at the headstone. She said: "Honey, I made the last payment on the house today, but nobody is there."

Houses are wonderful, but they can be so empty. Money is necessary, but it can't buy peace of soul. A new car is great, but when you lose a loved one, it doesn't give you much hope.

So, I say we need to learn the laughter of faith. It is very therapeutic. There CAN be laughter without faith, but faith ALWAYS produces laughter. I say again—it's difficult to have faith and worry foolishly at the same time.

We who call ourselves Christians can be so dumpy, grumpy and so humorless. The world doesn't need "dumpy" people, those who are always looking on the negative side of life. How we need to let God stretch our faith to the laughing point. We are not victims as long as we can laugh and see the positive side of life.

And let me add that preachers and churches don't need to add to our worries. I try to stay away from preachers who are always judging, condemning and scaring the hell out of people because of their horrible sins. We forget that Jesus said, "I've come NOT to condemn the world." Also, "Judge not but you be not judged." What part of that don't we understand? It's hard to be at peace when you're scared to death, or being told how bad we are.

Amen brothers and sisters, and now let the ushers come forward.

YOUR SOUL IS A WORK
IN PROGRESS

Forgive me for this old corny joke: Bill went to his female barber (named Grace) for a shave and haircut. The next morning, his face was as smooth as silk, and it was that way morning after morning. Just slick as glass. When Bill's wife called attention to it, Bill responded, "When you're shaved by Grace, once shaved, always shaved."

Come to think of it, I believe the Grace of God DOES indeed save me from many of life's difficult situations if I choose to receive it. But I also believe I have to continue working at it. The soul doesn't automatically grow itself. It's an every-day walk with God, an everyday trial and error. And the good news is that the errors become opportunities for the soul to grow. Who knowsthe person who experiences divorce, alcoholism, poverty and other such challenges, may be the wisest and most spiritual among us. Our neuroses, despair and failures are not at odds with the soul at all. In fact, these may be essential for the soul to grow and develop. Without negatives factors, life would be bland, insipid and undesirable. That's the "yin and yang" of life.

I believe that modem conveniences have taken much of the soul out of life. We can go through a day's routine without reflecting very deeply on anything. I can see that making bread is more soulful than buying bread. Working in your garden is more soulful than someone else doing it. It's more tiring but far more satisfying. Being tired can be a good thing. It's the creativity that makes the difference. So much is so prepackaged for us today that we may be losing the creative spirit.

The poet Keats said that the world is the "vale of soul-making." The soul reveals itself through the things that capture our imagination, time and energy. Sometimes, my soul talks back to me. "You're neglecting me. You need to stop and meditate and look at a tree and pray awhile. Stop 'doing' and enjoy 'being.'" The soul nudges me to slow down and enjoy the simple things of life, and be delivered from the hectic, stressful, demanding schedules we impose on ourselves. The soul is not interested in status, money, prestige, labels, and all the "-isms" floating around. It doesn't draw religious lines nor does it judge those who do. The soul emerges when we discover our individual uniqueness, with all of its beauty as well as its ugliness and craziness. It helps us to know the full depths of joy as well as pain.

Parents can help their children to grow their souls by giving them good positive scripts, such as "You can do it," or "Good job," "I'm proud of you," "You have what it takes." If a child hears "You'll never amount to anything," or "You are dumb or stupid," etc. the soul begins to wither.

The soul is never judgmental. And it is not impressed with denominationalism, titles, degrees, dogmatic beliefs or rigid rules. It respects tradition and seeks to grow from it, but it also cherishes freedom of choice, unity, silence, harmony and peace. It thrives on unselfish love and graceful giving. It sees all people as children of the creative God.

Jesus didn't talk about church buildings, theological opinions, rituals or creeds. He went about loving people, and emphasizing the importance of a good relationship with God and with each other. He talked about things of the spirit. "What shall it profit a man if he shall gain the whole world, and lose his own soul? (Mark 8:36)

Soul-making must also take into consideration what it means to live on the soil, consume clean water and air, and interact with ALL living things on this planet. A great part of the soul is outside the body. When our surroundings (oceans, rivers, air, forests and soils) are restored to health, our souls become healthier. We cannot go through life "for our own selfish benefit" without doing damage to the Spirit within.

So, your soul and mine are works in progress. It's a daily walk with God.

The prophet Jeremiah mentioned the "soul as a watered garden." (Jeremiah 31:12). Gardens need constant attention, and so does the Spirit. For when we come to the end of our days on this planet, we're stuck with it forever. Amen.

Life may not be tied with a bow, but it's still a gift.

HAPPINESS WITHOUT GUILT

"I feel so happy that I feel guilty," remarked a friend when asked how he was getting along.

Can you identify with that? Do we have a right to be happy, despite the fears, suffering and uncertainty in a world like ours? I believe so.

I believe very strongly that we are created to enjoy life to the fullest. I don't believe we do God (or anyone else) any favors by adding to the stockpile of misery in the world. I can participate in the suffering of others without forfeiting my own sense of well-being.

I realize, of course, that we cannot maintain an elevated mood of happiness ALL the time. Negative situations and painful experiences entitle me the right to feel sad. Also, if I listen to a depressed feeling, I may be able to identify and cope constructively with the culprit that caused it.

Researchers tell us, "Happiness can be learned and cultivated, and is not the sole product of genes, luck or delusions.

Also, researchers tell us what ISN'T making people happy. Money, intelligence, fame, prestige, or sunny weather. These things can bring moments of pleasure, but people get accustomed to new climates, higher salaries, and better cars. The novelty may fade and the basic problems remain, such as family conflicts, marital discord or the feeling that you are unloved.

So, what works? After more than a half century of pastoral ministry, I believe family closeness, genuine friendships, spiritual foundations, self-esteem and having worthwhile goals add to the happiness formula. And I am sure there's much more. Some seem to be born with an optimistic or happy gene. Pessimists are seldom very happy.

I heard a psychologist remark, "Activities come before feelings." That is, I need to do something every day that makes me feel good about myself, my relationship with God and with others. I need goals that are productive, but I don't need to make myself unhappy if I don't always reach them. It is pointless to try to convince myself that I SHOULD not feel frustrated over certain issues. Our shoulds and ought can add to our misery.

I find happiness in many ways, such as trying to see the funny side of life and enjoying much laughter. I feel happier when I exercise regularly and observe the other rules of good health. I find much joy by having strong support systems, such as my family, the church, and other groups with whom I share common interests. Unselfishly serving others bring about very positive feelings. Also, I try to remind myself that a grateful heart is seldom down in the dumps, and I try to remember to give thanks each day for endless blessings.

It is important for me also to focus on the "now" and to avoid going into the future or the past. The now is all we have, and when the future comes, it will just be a now again. I can cope with the now.

One other thought. I know from experience that I can make myself miserable with poor choices. I can needlessly produce feelings of sadness and self-downing by telling myself silly, irrational beliefs. I can allow "thought attacks" to destroy my peace of mind. What I tell myself about any given situation determines the way I feel.

So be good to yourself. And remember that you don't help anyone by going through life with long faces and negative feelings. Give yourself permission to be happy—without guilt.

A little girl sent this note to her teacher: "If you're happy, please tell your face." Amen.

NEGATIVE THINKING CAN PULL YOU DOWN—WAY DOWN

On a very hot day our electricity went out and stayed out for several hours. By the time it was dark, my wife had candles all over the house. "Now isn't this cozy and romantic?" she asked. I groaned: "Somehow it hasn't hit me yet."

Two people can have exactly the same experience and react miles apart. It's like seeing the glass half full or half empty. It seems that some people are born in the "objective case" and see the glass half empty. All of us make choices daily on how to react to any given situation.

Do you know someone who is negative about almost everything? Like the woman who was sick and her friend asked her how she was doing. "I'm a little better now," she said. "That's good," her friend smiled. "Oh no, I've discovered that I always feel WORSE right after I get to feeling better," moaned the woman. We can "awfulize" any situation to the point of illness.

One of most dangerous forms of negative thinking is to be in denial of a problem that you alone can correct. How many marriages end in divorce because of denying a habit one may have? When you deny the truth about yourself instead of admitting you need help, life can fall apart in a hurry.

Negative thinking is like poison that reaches into every part of being. Norman Vincent Peale advocated positive thinking all during his ministry and the longer I live, the more respect I have for him. Good mental AND physical health depends upon positive thinking. There is nothing "Pollyanna" or hiding your head in the sand" about it. It's choosing to find something good in every situation and acting on that belief.

I was so impressed with a Boston Marathon runner who lost a leg in the bombing. He said during an interview: "I still have so much to be thankful for. And even though I lost a leg, I can still see, and taste good food, and enjoy my family and friends and one day I'll run again." He is making the best out of a bad situation.

If there is one thing that stands out in reading the Scriptures, it is that NO ONE can USE the power God gave you. Some people use this power, this ability to overcome an addiction or to persevere while others sink in despair. When the Disciples asked Jesus about how many times to forgive, Jesus answered, "I don't say seven times, but seventy times seven." Living with a grudge can sap your strength as well as having an impact on your blood pressure, etc. Positive thinking makes good blood.

According to an old Hindu legend, there was a time when all people were gods. People abused their divinity so the chief god decided to take away their divinity and hide it. Where? Deep in the ocean? No. High on a mountain? No, it can't be found there either. They decided to hide it deep inside human beings because they will never think to look for it there. Ever since, we have been climbing, digging and diving for something which is already inside. Jesus said "The Kingdom of God is not coming with signs, but the Kingdom is within." The Kingdom means fulfillment, happiness, and peace.

During the days of Jesus people looked for signs outside themselves for God. I confess that I have upon occasion, asked God to give me a sign. But Jesus gave us this insight: "Blessed are the pure in heart, for they shall see God." Blessed are those who hunger for righteousness, for they shall be filled. Blessed are the merciful..." and so on. See Matthew 5 for the Beatitudes.

Another thing about positive thinking is that it helps us to grow. We have the power to change and to follow our dreams in life. Some folks take the opposite side by playing the blame game. We can blame our circumstances on our upbringing. Or bad luck. We can play "If only_____" or "What if _____?" or "If it hadn't been for her/him_____."

Also, we need to stop thinking that we have to be perfect to live in God's Kingdom. Jesus looked at the imperfect Pharisees and said "The Kingdom is in your midst." In other words, we can live in the Kingdom as a sinner, as long as we don't accept our sin as something that defines us.

We need to accept our humanity. Jesus was human, tempted as we are. They accused him of being a wine bibber, a glutton and one who healed on the Sabbath. Yet, his positive outlook on life helped him to forgive those who put him on Cross.

Finally, I think about Joseph in the Old Testament. He had every reason to be bitter, and revengeful. He could have let hatred eat him up, because his brothers sold him into Egyptian slavery. Yet he was optimistic enough to turn a bad situation into something good. (See Genesis 37). Joseph's dreams came true and he became a ruler in Egypt.

So beware of negative thinking. It certainly can pull you down—way down. These days call for a strong faith in the power of God plus the power of your will-power.

I close with the words of the late Grace Sandefur, who lived to be in her nineties: "I cast my burden upon the waters and it came back bread."

A LITTLE RELIGION
IS A DANGEROUS THING

I visited a man one day who seemed very ill at ease. Fumbling for words, he said rather apologetically, "I'm not a very religious person."

My immediate response was, "Good, I don't believe God calls us to be 'religious.'" He looked puzzled, but I continued: "The more I study Scriptures, the more I see that we are called to a way of life, a way of relating to each other, to ourselves, our families, the world around us, and to God."

It's easy to get "hung up" over religion, to worship the container rather than the content, to value the nets more than the fish, and to allow the trappings of religious symbols, rituals, creeds and doctrines to become a substitute for a vital relationship with the God of ALL creation. Religiosity (the way we go about worship) can be a sure way to avoid a deep spirituality, a hindrance to living the gospel in everyday life where decisions, behavior, speech and motives really matter.

History tells us that people have done any terrible and demonic things in the name of "religion." Much trouble in the world today relates to belief systems. Beliefs can separate families, nations, and neighbors. This ought not to be so.

Will we ever see and understand that all of us are inter-related, regardless of our religious labels. We are all connected to the family of God, despite our differences.

So, a little religion is a dangerous thing if it leads us to believe that our "brand" is the ONLY brand of religion. We simply do not have God in our back pockets.

God is clearly beyond human comprehension. Any image or idea of God falls short of the reality of God. It seems to me that "God is Creative Love" is about as close as we can get.

We can be so conditioned or blinded by our culture or religious heritage that we only see and believe what we've been taught. We need to make room for other possibilities. To use a modern cliché, we need to "think outside the box—the theological box."

Salvation or enlightenment is not something we do. It is something we experience when we become free of all prejudices, judgments, and labels. We must become EMPTY for God's love to fill us.

A little religion is a dangerous thing if we have just enough to make us feel guilty, and not enough to accept God's forgiving Grace. As long as we hold to a reward-punishment belief system, this will be true. Religion has gone bad if it gives us more guilt than Grace.

May God help us, then, to accept God's Grace, and to live and help live regardless of our religious boxes. Let us find not only the words, but also the music. For as St. Paul wrote to the Romans (5:20) "Where sin abounds, grace does more abound." Amen

WAYS TO WRINKLE YOUR SOUL

A friend handed me this quote by an unknown author:

"Youth is not a time of life; it is a state of mind.
Years wrinkle the skin, but to give up enthusiasm wrinkles the soul."

"Enthusiasm" comes from the word "en theos," which means "in God."
It is the ONE thing we need to keep strong throughout life, for to lose it will definitely wrinkle the soul.

There are proven ways we can do this.

First, by becoming cynical and pessimistic. Some people have a "failure syndrome." "Nothing works." "It's hopeless." "What's the use?" I heard someone say that her father had a "damn the luck" philosophy but her mother had a "count your blessings" outlook.

Another way to wrinkle the soul is by living with a grudge. Someone disappointed you, or said hateful words, and you can't turn it loose. You nurture it and feed it with negative thoughts. You give them power over you, allowing them to control your emotions. Thus, you end up punishing yourself and nothing is gained. Your soul cries out for peace.

There are many ways to wrinkle your soul, but let me mention one more. And that is to fret about aging and to constantly tell yourself how bad you look and feel. I know people who are constantly giving themselves a hard time because they can't do the things they once did or look the way they once looked.

A young man on crutches who had been stricken by a crippling disease was asked the question, "How can you be so happy and face everything with such enthusiasm?" His quick reply was, "Oh, that's easy. The disease didn't affect my heart."

Finally, I leave you with a wonderful quote from Joel Osteen's book *Becoming a Better You* (p.111): "It's important that we get into the habit of declaring good things over our lives every day. When you get up in the morning, instead of looking at that mirror and saying, "Oh, I can't believe I look like this. I'm getting so old, so wrinkled," you need to smile and say, "Good morning, you good-looking thing... God is renewing my strength like the eagles and I am excited about life."

Amen.

GOD WRITES STRAIGHT
WITH CROOKED LINES

I remember a movie some time ago filmed on a Louisiana plantation. It was the story of a prostitute who was able to help a group of nuns save a Convent. The person of ill repute stood out as the heroine of the story, and in reference to her, someone quoted an old Spanish proverb: "God writes straight with crooked lines."

I've thought about this many times and how it applies to so much of life. After deciding to go into the ministry, I experienced a real sense of inadequacy. I thought, "Who am I to stand in the pulpit and try to interpret God's Word to the people?"

I shared these feelings with a friend, whose response put it in perspective: "Don't worry," he said, "you are inadequate, and will always be. If God had to wait until a perfect person comes along to be in ministry, God's work would never get done."

God can and does use unlikely people to get the job done, despite our blunders, sins and mistakes.

St. Benedict of the 6th century is best known for having written the Benedictine Rule, which is a simple statement of the Christian faith. The Rule is the belief that "God is everywhere, all the time and thus every element of our ordinary day is potentially holy."

This is a challenge for each of us, and involves a life-long response. All are potentially holy - good, patient, kind, loving, etc. This gives me hope.

So it is safe to say that all of the popes, preachers, priests, rabbis, gurus, and teachers who have ever lived could join this inadequate fraternity of servants. To be human is to be imperfect.

I remember a parishioner named Joe, who was a rough and tough customer, and his language was rated R most of the time. Yet, Joe had a heart of gold and would do anything to help people in the community. He looked after several widows by becoming a handyman. When he came to church, no one wanted to sit close to him because he was far from being cologned. And when he sang, his gravel voice was excruciating. But I believe he did more Christian deeds than anyone in that congregation. Joe was my hero. God writes straight with crooked lines.

People like Joe have helped me to believe in the basic goodness of human nature. I believe most of us are better than we think we are. All we have to do is to claim God's Mercy and Grace and serve the best way we can. We are the twinkle in God's eye.

I agree with the words of Max Ehrmann's *Desiderata*:

"You are a child of the Universe, no less than the trees and the stars. You have a right to be here. And whether it is clear to you, no doubt the Universe is unfolding as it should. Therefore be at peace with yourself and with God, whatever you conceive God to be." Amen.

DEALING WITH DEMONS

The TV comedian said: "The devil made me do it," and we laughed.

A recent newspaper had an account of a 16 year-old who broke into the home of an elderly couple, robbed them and beat them unmercifully. The teenager was caught and arrested, and said he did it "just for kicks." Psychiatrists explained that he was "outside himself," split away from the real person he usually was, which was kind and congenial. Neighbors said DEMONS or the devil got into him and caused him to do it.

Is there some "demonic" force that CAUSES people to behave in such destructive ways? Where do these demons originate? In other words, are we at the mercy of some entity outside ourselves, completely removed from our freedom of choice? I don't think so.

I contend there was NO force outside that young man that caused him to brutally attack that elderly couple. Unless a person is completely psychotic, removed from reality, incoherent or brain damaged, that person is capable of being *responsible* for his or her actions. A person does not have to turn into the incarnation of a so-called devil or Satan. These are delusions born out of our own destructive thought pattern or moral weakness.

The root word for Satan is "adversary." Who can deny the existence of adversaries, such as greed, envy, selfishness, or fear? I suppose we all have our demons. Jesus called them "legion." So when I name them, I can deal with them more effectively.

The Apostle Paul in the New Testament wrote, "For we are not contending with flesh and blood, but against the principalities, against the power, against the rulers of this present darkness, against the spiritual hosts of wickedness in heavenly places." (Ephesians 6:12)

Satan is pictured as a fictional character in Goethe's Faust with a long tail, cloven hoofs, horns, and carrying a pitchfork. He is called the Prince of Darkness, Beelzebub, the Keeper of Hell's Gates, and a number of other names. Lesser devils are referred to as demons, who scout around seeking un-suspecting people or victims.

There is another story of Satan being cast out of Heaven for disobedi-ence. Becoming a fallen angel, this Satan roams around the earth as an evil force beyond God's control. Milton's Lucifer in <u>Paradise Lost</u> follows this theme. Again, it is wholly fictional.

The point I'm leading up to is this: I believe in the exclusive power of ONE God, who is the Lord and Creator of the Universe, and does not share the universal stage with an equally powerful force called Satan.

So, the evil spirit is WITHIN us, not hiding in some bush somewhere ready to attack. One of the things they said about Jesus of Nazareth was "He cast out demons." This was not some magical trick. He simply touched people at the point of their need, helping them to become WHOLE again, and to stop acting crazy, hurting themselves as well as others. He didn't use the devil as a scapegoat for the wrongdoing that people chose to do.

To summarize: When any of our natural urges or drives get out of hand, such as sex, hunger, or anger, the results can be disastrous, and demonic. But as long as we have the gift of FREE will, we don't have to allow these drives to take over and wreak havoc. So thanks be to God for freedom of choice, for the power to choose right over wrong, and the ability to take the high road.

"The devil made me do it," quipped Flip Wilson, but I didn't believe a word of it.

COPING WITH LOSS

Everyone experiences loss. It is part of the human scene. We encounter it very early in life with the death of a pet. How many times I have stood in the back yard with one or more of our children to say a prayer of thanksgiving over the grave of a dog or some other animal!

We experience loss also because of poor choices and carelessness. We may lose relationships because of distance, disappointment or divorce. With every passage in life, we have to deal with loss and make adjustments. As I write this, Hurricane Katrina is causing many losses to New Orleans, the Gulf Coast and other areas. There will be loss of homes and loss of life.

Surely the most painful loss is the death of a loved one. We are human enough to want to hold on to those we love. This loss makes other losses seem almost insignificant by comparison. Our first grandchild, only 32, lost his struggle with a brain tumor after struggling more than eight years.

At such a traumatic time, it helped me to turn to the book of Job in the Old Testament. Job lost EVERYTHING he had treasured: his family, farm, health and wealth. Only one thing was left and that was the certainty that he didn't deserve it. It wasn't fair. It wasn't right. Job's condition was so miserable that his wife encouraged him to curse God and die. However, he scolds her and accepts his situation standing tall. He refuses to turn away from God, although his so-called friends weren't any more help to him and his wife. Job continued to believe in the ultimate justice of God and remarked, "Though He slay me, yet will I trust Him.

Believing in the ultimate goodness and righteousness of God, Job finally uttered this great statement of faith:

"For I know that my Redeemer lives,
And at last He will stand upon the Earth,
And after my skin has been destroyed,
Then from my flesh shall I see God."

There are so many good and noble people like Job who have suffered and will continue to do so. We have watched friends and family members suffer with unbearable burdens. We have all witnessed tragedies.

One of the hardest things I ever did, as a pastor, was to tell a young teenager that her only brother and parents had been killed in a plane crash. "It's not fair," I thought, "It's not right." And I certainly didn't believe it to be God's will that my grandson die at such an early age. Yet, I stand on the edge of ignorance with St. Paul who said, "Now we see through a glass darkly." At our grandson's memorial service, a friend read "The Serenity Prayer', by Reinhold Nielbuhr

"Lord, help me to accept the things I cannot change, the courage to change the things I can, and the wisdom to know the difference." (Paraphrased)

So, this must be the way to cope with loss: Learn to accept the things we cannot change. And after we have done the best we can to change the situation, we commit it to God's care.

During the Second World War in Britain, a certain church in London was set for its harvest festival. People brought their fruit and vegetables and placed them around the altar. It was Saturday night so that everything would be in place for worship the next morning. They never had their harvest celebration, however. That very night, the church was bombed and left in ruins. Weeks passed, winter came, and then spring, and someone noticed little shoots of green on the bomb site where the church had stood. The shoots flourished. After a while, there was a healthy patch of wheat growing in the middle of the rubble. The bombs and destruction had not taken the life out of the wheat!

Isn't this a parable of what God can do in our lives? Unless the seed dies, a new plant cannot be born. No matter how many difficult blows life can deal us, we have hope. And we are surrounded by the loving support of family and friends.

I leave you this month with this old Hymn that expresses it well:

"This is my Father's world,
O let me ne'er forget,
That though the wrong seems oft so strong,
God is the ruler yet."(MD Babcock 1901, Methodist Hymnal, page 144)

When the student is ready, the teacher will arrive.

MAKING PEACE
WITH OUR PASSAGES

Life has a way of confronting us with passages all along the way. When finished with one passage, another is approaching. And sometime we experience much grief and frustration.

How we need to make peace with these ever changing life situations.

In the Old Testament, the writer of Ecclesiastes said that the Lord has made everything beautiful in its time. "There is a time for everything: a time to be born and a time to die, a time to weep and a time to laugh; a time to mourn and a time to dance." (See Ecclesiastes 3:1-11) Everything has its time.

TIME is a mystery and a great gift. I have never really understood it, especially as I grow older and it seems to be galloping at an ever increasing rate. I can't slow it down, but I CAN lean into it and make the most of it.

The Psalmist once said: "So teach us to number our days that we may get a wise heart." (Psalms 90:12)

A wise heart is one that makes peace with the passing of time and the many changes occurring. A wise heart accepts what is, and realizes we are not in control. Sometimes we feel like Charlie Brown, who said, "I feel like I'm a chocolate ice cream kid living in a broccoli world."

I. A Wise Heart Accepts The Permanence of Change.

In 1899, Charles Duel, Director of the U.S. Patent Office, said: "Everything that CAN be invented has been invented." Think of the changes since this statement was made.

Too much change too fast disturbs us unless we are prepared to go with the flow.

I'll never forget when our first-born daughter was married. Everything went as planned until I saw Becky coming down the aisle on her grandfather's arm. A throat-frog popped up and I couldn't swallow. I broke out in a cold sweat, and to this day, I don't know how I made it through the ceremony. For I knew our little girl had grown up and things would never be the same at our house. What I didn't know was that things would be even better. For we gained a fine son-in-law, three wonderful grandchildren and five beautiful great-grandchildren. But you see, if it had been left to me, I would have kept her at home.

So we can RANT and RAVE and make ourselves sick, or we can accept the changes of life by the Grace of God, and move on.

Sociologists talk about the revolutionary changes in the last half of the 20th century. It seems that all the structures of the society are breaking down. Someone put it this way: "Everything nailed down is coming loose." This is one reason we are experiencing a world-wide fundamentalist movement, which affects religion, politics and just about everything else. Fundamentalism is the human reaction to too much change too soon. Yet, unless we change, we don't learn and we don't grow.

"God made everything beautiful in its time," said the writer of Ecclesiastes. Hopefully we can move toward God's will in all of our changes.

II. A Wise Heart Nurtures Relationships Today, knowing that one day, we will have to let go.

This is difficult, because we tend to become possessive of loved ones. We BOND with family and friends; we eat with them, laugh with them, share life itself with them, and then it's over.

So NOW is the time to nurture your relationships with lots of TLC. Don't put it off.

III. A Wise Heart Makes Peace with the Ultimate Passage, which is death of the physical body. It happens to each of us.

"We are not ready to live unless we are prepared to die," said an old sage. But the problem is that we find it easy to be overly attached to this world. We can over-identify with this world so much that we give little or no thought to the next dimension. Physical death is part of God's plan. I'm not referring to premature death from natural disaster; I'm talking about death at the end of a normal life span.

I heard about a monk who watched his barn burn down, and remarked, "Oh, good, now I can see the moon." Sooner or later we will have to let go of our barns, material things, houses, cars, money and the people we love most.

But this will be our ultimate freedom. The soul will be set free from an imperfect body. The soul will find a spiritual body, as it returns to God.

Yes, the cemetery speaks to us:

If you have anything to do, do it now.
If you have anything to say, say it now.
If you have any apologies to make, make them now.
If you have anyone to love, love them now.
Let's make peace with our passages, trusting God with things present and
    things to come.
It's the only way to travel!

WHEN LIFE IS A DRAG, YOU DO HAVE THE POWER TO COPE!

I believe most of us have more "coping" power than we realize. It is said that all behavior is learned behavior. So we can choose to be positive or negative; we can build up or tear down; we can help or we can hinder. It's an old cliché, but life IS what you make it.

There used to be a popular song, "Everything is beautiful," and to a large degree, this is true. There is beauty everywhere if we have eyes that "see," especially this time of the year when the miracles of growth are popping up all around us.

But to multitudes, life is not very beautiful. Because of poverty, lack of opportunities, tragedies, dysfunctional relationships or whatever, to many, life is a drag. A downer. A test of endurance. I was talking with a friend recently and age came into our conversation. I asked her, "How long would you like to live if you had your choice?" She quickly answered, "Not a whole lot longer, I'm getting tired of this mess." Was I shocked! I thought she had everything to be happy about and to live for. You never know by looking at a person what's going on in their inner being.

In the 42nd Psalm (10-11) we find these words, "Why are you cast down, O my soul, why are you disquieted within in me?" The "dark night of the soul" was very familiar to the Psalmist.

Paul Tillich tells about a doctor who was treating a deeply depressed patient. "You need a little amusement and you need to laugh. Go see the circus clown, Grimaldi, he will make you laugh. The patient looked at him: "My Lord, doctor, I AM Grimaldi." I suppose there are times when putting up a front and smiling hides the way we actually feel. There's an old saying, "Fake it 'til you make it." Yet, that's trying to force your mood, which may or may not work. I went to see my family doctor years ago because I felt lousy. He told me that I should go fishing. I took his advice, but I felt the same way fishing. I had to get to the bottom of my problem before I could move on. If you listen to your depression long enough, it will tell you what's wrong.

A friend said, "I feel so uptight lately that I can't even go to sleep in church." As God's people we give the impression that we need to be happy all the time, and the truth is, we don't. Some folks feel as if they have failed or they lack enough faith if they feel miserable. That's simply not true. Being depressed is not a weakness. It can be treated.

So let me share some observations with you.

First, don't be afraid of your feelings because feelings are not always facts. (I can feel like there's a burglar in the kitchen when it may be the cat turned something over.) Sometimes our feelings can conjure up all kinds of trouble when reality tells us differently. You may have the feeling that nobody loves you, but that's hardly the case.

Yet we need to listen to our feelings because they may be telling us to slow down, or to make a change or to learn how to pray. The Psalmist said, "My tears have been my meat, my food, day and night." (42:3) Living off of tears? Not much of a diet, I'd say. Of course, there are times when we need to let go and wash it out. Tears can wash out the toxins very well, but we need to move on. A friend said to me, "If there were no tears, there would be no rainbows."

After my first wife passed away, I recalled that she had said many times, "If something happens to me, please go on living." It was very difficult at first but I refused to give up my right to live as long as I could and not dwell on the past. As I have said many times, "don't stumble on anything behind you. If it's gone, move on." God has blessed me with a new lease on life, but I had to do my part.

Not long ago, I read about what the University of Texas students do during finals. They find an old car and, with baseball bats or clubs, they beat the car to a pulp, screaming, ranting and raving. They said that's the best way to get rid of stress. I think most of us have to find a way to relieve tension. I do it by working in my garden. The worst thing you can do is to sit around and mope.

Another observation is, "Accept help from people you can trust." Talk to them when you are feeling low. I believe it really helps to ventilate our feelings but you can't do this with just anybody. We need trusted friends who are willing to listen to us and pray with us. Everyone needs a little help at times.

I went to see a good friend in the hospital one day. She had just been told that she had an inoperable malignancy. She said, "I know no one can take this from me—will you just hold my hand and pray?" I did more than that. I put my arms around her and we both wept. When you don't know what to say to a friend who is in deep trouble, remember that one of the best things you can do is simply the gift of presence. Just be there. Sometimes, words aren't necessary.

When Jesus was facing the cross, he didn't want to die because his ministry had just begun. He prayed, "Father, if it be possible, let this cup pass from me." Even his closest friends went to sleep and wouldn't stay up with him one hour. He was denied and betrayed by his best friends. He agonized and suffered alone and great drops of blood felt from his skin. Then he said, "Not my will but thine be done." He allowed God to use the Cross to show that God so loved the world that he gave his only begotten son that whosoever believed in him would not perish but have everlasting life." Amen.

IF I'VE GOT IT MADE,
WHY AM I SO MISERABLE?

When folks say, "I've got it made," I assume they are referring to material success. At least, that's what a friend meant when he uttered those words to me. Everything "John" touched turned to money. He inherited a lucrative business and expanded it to the point of becoming a multi-millionaire. One evening, when we were visiting on his patio, I congratulated him on his achievements, and he jarred me with this comment: "If I've got it made, why am I so miserable? Something is missing in my life and I don't know what it is."

We talked at length and I tried to help him discover the source of his emptiness. It all had to do with his lack of purpose; the total neglect of spiritual goals and very little enlightened awareness. Dr. Carl Yung, Swiss physician, wrote a lot about the "afternoon" of life, or what we may call "the mid-life crisis." He says this is where many people bog down. I believe this is where my friend was. He had succeeded in his business life by the age of 48, but had neglected his personal relationship with his family and with God. He had reached the age of boredom and felt dead inside.

It reminded me of the words in the New Testament: "What will it profit a man if he should gain the whole world and lose his own soul?" [Mark 8:36} "John" had taken good care of his material needs but had overlooked the things of the spirit. He had put his soul "on hold."

I believe there are four levels of awareness. And it is likely that most of us go in and out of these levels at different times in life.

The first is Simple Awareness. This person looks at a mountain and thinks it is a nice mountain. He finds happiness in the natural beauty of the world and in his own inner world. He is not driven in pursuit of goals constantly. He's just happy to live and let live. It's the "Garden of Eden" life, which is rather rare in our society.

The second level is Complicated Awareness. Those on this level may look at a mountain, but they are afraid to get near it because there may be snakes under the rocks, and it also may contain a volcano. They spend much time worrying and being in a state of anxiety over the dangers of the mountain. They live by fear, which describes a lot of people in our Western culture. They push their children out of the "Garden of Eden" too soon in an effort for them to excel in some endeavor, thus robbing their offspring of their childhood. Our pressured and stressful lifestyle has all but obliterated simple awareness from our lives.

The third level is Consumer Awareness. These people look at a mountain and wonder how they can own that piece of property to turn it into a profit. They would clear the trees, sell the timber and create a new sub-division. Consumer awareness seeks personal gain, and sees the dollar mark almost everywhere. They may trade their soul for a mess of pottage. (I believe this is where my friend was. He had it made, but the mountain no longer gave him satisfaction. He had consumed it and there was nothing left.)

Then, there is the fourth and more desired level, Enlightened Awareness. It is akin to Simple Awareness, but it goes a few steps beyond. On this level, people see the mountain and behold the beauty and mystery of it all. They may write poetry, paint pictures, sing songs or just meditate on this mountain. They may even have a transcending experience on top of it. They will invite their family and friends to share in the beauty and joy of this great handiwork of God. They feel blessed just to be near it.

William Randolph Hearst was a wealthy newspaperman. One day, he saw a copy of a painting he liked very much. He wanted the original, so he hired a private detective to find it, regardless of the cost. Finally, the detective told him that he had found the painting in, of all places, his own warehouse. Hearst unwittingly already owned it! I believe this story is a parable for all of us today. The things we want most are right under our noses, and we are either too asleep or too unaware to really see it and appreciate it. We have family, friends and a world of beauty and blessings right at our fingertips, but we may be all the while blind to this reality.

I will close with these words from Psalm 121: (NRV)

"I will lift mine eyes to the hills,
From whence does my help come?
My help comes from the Lord,
Who made heaven and earth.
The Lord will keep you from all evil;
He will keep your life.
The Lord will keep your going out and you're coming in
From this time forth and forever. Amen."

LIVING A QUALITY LIFE

I'd venture to say that most of us want a quality life! We want to enjoy our time on Earth, and we go to great lengths to do so. I'm one of those people who don't want to miss a thing. I called a friend the other day right after lunchtime, and said, "I hope I didn't disturb your nap." She quickly responded, "I don't take naps—I'm afraid I'll miss something." That's me.

However, we are living in a day when medical science is keeping a person alive long after quality of life has disappeared. I was with a family recently, and their loved one was alive only because of artificial means. They finally realized that they needed to withdraw support, and let nature take its course. This is always a difficult decision, to say the least.

On the other hand, it seems almost cruel to keep a person's body alive long after they have lost the ability to enjoy life. This is the reason many have drawn up a "Living Will," and I believe everybody needs one. As much as we hesitate to think about it, death is a fact of life, and part of God's plan. There comes a time when our bodies are no longer useful to us, and God has provided a way to vacate them. Yet, knowing all of this, there is a fundamental anxiety about dying, leaving family members and friends and the world as we know it.

Not many of us are like the woman I read about recently. She felt her time was limited, so she went to the funeral home and asked the director if she could look at the caskets. She asked to see a blue one, lined with pink. After locating the one she wanted, she asked if she could get into it to see how it felt. A friend commented as she settled in, "Mable, this is YOU!" Most of us are not that relaxed with our departure.

Now, having said these things, let me try to define a quality life. I realize that this varies according to individual tastes, but let me raise three questions. You will notice that none of these refer to material possessions, although it's no fun to be poor. But, quality of life transcends our material blessings. As Jesus put it, "A person's life does not consist in the abundance of his possessions."

The first question is, do you anticipate life each day, or do you think, "Just my rotten luck—ANOTHER day?" Do you dread getting out of bed in the morning? There is a song by Dory Previn, titled The Game. He compares life to a roulette wheel, implying that we can't win. His words: "Pilate's soldiers gambled at the foot of the cross, even for the ragged robe that was lost, so would ya care to tell me boss, what chance have we?" Is life rigged? Is it a never-ending joke? Well, I don't believe so.

I believe there are two classes of people: Those who MAKE things happen and those who WAIT for things to happen. Some are waiting for a miracle to come along and carry them into "happy land," anything to take them out of their boredom, loneliness and frustration. A friend said to me, "Nobody knows what I'm going through, and I don't feel at home in this world anymore." Shortly thereafter, she died. I believe this case only illustrates that we can, indeed, will ourselves to death.

The second question is, are you giving your life to anyone else? We are either adding to, or taking from, another person's life all the time. A woman once wrote to Ann Landers: "Don't I have the right to nag my husband when he overeats?" Ann replied, "Nagging has probably killed more marriages than over-eating ever has." In this way, we can give death to another person, especially through nagging, jealousy, unfaithfulness and criticism.

The final question I want to raise is, are you making a spiritual connection? Our relationship with God is so important. Each of us has to make our own connection. Faith is a personal matter. There's no ONE road to spiritual fulfillment. Likewise, to think we have the ONLY answer to salvation is pure self-righteousness. It was Garrison Keiler of Wobegone, Minnesota who said, "If you believe in a loving and merciful God, life is a comedy and you might as well enjoy it, and quit worrying." Comedy—not as in a joke, but comedy in the Shakespearean sense. In tragedy, everything turns out badly, and we worry about it. But, in comedy, all's well that ends well, and we enjoy it. In this context, the Gospel is far more comedy than tragedy. For Jesus said, "Let not your hearts be troubled, neither let them be afraid."(John 14:1)

You cannot change anyone but yourself.

YOU ARE CHOSEN

Whoever said that we are blessed to be a blessing, knew what they were talking about. This strikes at the very heart of our mission as people of God. If we are blessed and do not bless others, we become a dead-end street, or like the Dead Sea. All of us can be conduits of life's blessing.

In the play *Fiddler on the Roof*, Tevye said, "I know we are chosen," as he looked toward Heaven, "but I wish you wouldn't choose us so often." Being chosen however is often misunderstood, especially if we interpret it to mean that we are superior or favored, a cut above the rest. There is too much of the "we-they" attitude in the world as it is. In one sense, most of us enjoy the concept of being chosen, or being number 1, the winner, the champion. And we symbolize this with gold medals, blue ribbons, trophies and the like. There's nothing wrong with that. As one who dabbles in art, I enjoy it when one of my paintings snag a ribbon or recognition. It feels good, and it energizes me to keep going. But this also has its danger.

Jesus had trouble with his followers at this very point. They were caught up in the "me first" syndrome. In the 10th chapter of Mark, James and John went to Jesus asking that they be granted the honor of sitting one at his right hand and the other on his left hand in the coming of the Kingdom. Jesus must have smiled as he told them that they didn't know what they were asking for. He asked, "Can you drink from the cup that I am about to drink?" In other words, "Can you suffer the way I will suffer?" Then he says, "Whoever is first (greatest) among you is the servant of all." (Mark10:35-45)

So being chosen means that we have a job to do, a mission, a great responsibility. Let me unpack this with three statements. First, we are chosen to make a difference. As children of God, this is our calling. Matthew Arnold's famous quote is, "We should be ashamed to live and to die unless we have won some victory for humanity." As we turn to the scriptures, we find Moses being chosen to lead the children of Israel out of Egypt. Jeremiah was chosen to be a prophet, a spokesman for God. David was chosen to give God's message in songs and Psalms. All made a difference. We, too, can make a difference, where we are, with what we have, while there is time. It doesn't have to be something big. Sometimes, it's a kind word, a random deed or a simple prayer.

Secondly, we are chosen to be peacemakers. Isn't it ironic that the place where Jesus taught about love and peace, is today among the most troubled spots in the world? But we don't have to go to the Holy Land to find unholy behavior. Some people are troublemakers. They are judgmental, critical, and cruel. Such people are insensitive to the feelings of others.

Then we are chosen to be servants. I believe God has called us to be here for each other, regardless of race, creed, nationality, or religion. When Paul was in Macedonia, there arose a dispute, and people were angry with each other. He wrote that God had comforted them by the arrival of Titus. Titus was a "loyal child in the faith" (Titus: 1:4). He was a peacemaker, and a devoted servant. So, who is your Titus? Who helps you cope with difficult circumstances? Who offers hope, comfort and encouragement? When life falls apart, where do you find the strength to carry on?

Yes, all of us need the "Titus Touch," but most of all, we need to hear and abide by the words of Isaiah: "They that wait upon the Lord shall renew their strength, they shall mount up with wings as Eagles, they shall run and not be weary, they shall walk and not faint" (Isaiah 40:31)

WHY DO WE SUFFER?

A college student wrote the following to his parents:

"Dear Mom and Dad,
"Hope you are doing okay. You said go to church and wear clean socks. The socks I can take, but going to church bothers me. The Reverend is always talking about how good God is. I am thinking, well, why do kids starve, and disease cripples and why do tornadoes kill, and why are some babies born without a dog's chance? Oh well, I'm okay, and my socks are clean.
"Love, Tim."

If you received a letter like this, how would you respond?

The question of suffering is an old one, and there are no pat answers, to be sure.

Being human makes all of us vulnerable to suffering, no matter who we are. The rain falls on the just and unjust. (Matthew 5:45)

The word "suffer" comes from the Latin "to bear up" or "to endure." Some people have to endure a great deal in life.

We suffer for several reasons. Let me mention three.

1. **There is suffering that is self-inflicted**. This is very common. We can bring it on ourselves without a lot of effort. Sometimes I wish I didn't have so much "freedom of choice."

Take eating, for example. I can be at a great banquet and there is a feast before my eyes. And I want to try a little of everything. So I eat and eat. (It takes 7 minutes for the stomach to inform the brain that I've had enough). But by that time, it may be too late. My eyes bulge, my breath is short and I ask myself: WHY did I do it?

Our freedom of choice can get us into a lot of difficulty in so many ways. So, a lot of suffering is "home-made misery."

2. **Then, there suffering that is inflicted on us by others.** Think of all the atrocities that people are responsible for. Did you know that over 100 million people were killed by other people in the twentieth century alone? That's insanity!

Eckhart Tolle, author of the best-selling book *The Power of Now*, said that the human mind can be so diseased and polluted that it becomes our worst enemy. The egoistic mind collects insults and injuries of all sorts. Somehow, we must get in control of the mind, or it will control us. You are MORE than your mind. You are a SPIRIT being, and this Spirit needs to be in control of your life.

3. **Then, there is the suffering over which we have little or no control.** This can be the most difficult suffering of all. Hurricanes, tornadoes, earthquakes, etc. are in this category. God is sometimes blamed for this. Primitive religions pointed to this theory.

Shortly after the Columbia shuttle tragedy, someone asked: Why did God allow this to happen? I dare not try to speak for God, except to say that we live in a world of natural as well as spiritual laws. One of those natural laws is the law of gravity. Surely, God doesn't waive the natural law to accommodate our flying machines when they fall apart. I don't believe that God breaks His laws for our safety.

So, where does that leave us? It can leave us with resentment and bitterness, or we can learn to accept what we cannot change and learn from it.

Bernie Segal made this remark: "The world breaks everyone sooner or later, but some of us are stronger at the broken places."

Or as a friend said to me recently: "I am too blessed to be stressed and too anointed to be disappointed."

Amen.

Though my outer nature is wasting away, my inner nature is being renewed every day.

FINDING HEAVEN
IN THE HERE AND NOW

I remember a line from the movie, "Steel Magnolias," when M'linn had died as a young mother. At the cemetery following the Interment, one of her angry, grief-stricken friends said, "I feel like slapping SOMEBODY."

I suppose there are times when most of us feel that way. (As if that would make things better). But anger and grief are common feelings in a world like ours, where so many things don't make sense.

A friend said, "Happiness is a gift you give yourself." In today's world, we have to fight to be positive or optimistic or cheerful. It's easy for us to allow the news to engulf us to the point of depression and worry. We need not add to the stockpile of misery in the world. We are responsible for our own mental outlook, and although we cannot give happiness to anyone else, we CAN give them love, friendship and encouragement, especially during their loss. We don't realize how contagious attitudes can be.

I love this quote by Elizabeth Kübler-Ross: "People are like stained glass windows; they sparkle and shine when the sun's out, but when the darkness sets in, their true beauty is revealed only if there is light within."

To say that we live in a difficult and uncertain time is like saying that we live in a time when the sun comes up. From what little I know about the history, every age has had its set of challenges and uncertainties. Communication and technical skills increase our awareness of the negative and evil forces that exist. We can be so traumatized by the negative that we fail to find creative ways of coping. We can be so immersed in our own sorrows that we fail to see the BIG picture. Instead of asking, "WHY did this or that happen?" it is more appropriate to ask, "HOW can I get through this?" The word "why" can lead to a dead end street and endless frustration.

An American philosopher, Bernard Gert, identifies certain principles that will minimize misery and promote a more positive way of life. Here is a partial list: Don't cause pain, don't disable, don't deprive anyone of freedom or pleasure, don't deceive anyone, keep your promises, don't cheat, obey the law, do your duty and take responsibility. This reflects some of the basic truth of the Ten Commandments plus a lot of good common sense.

In Ken Olsen's satirical book, *Can You Wait Til Friday?*, is this story of a woman named Sarah, who was determined to quit living. She called Olsen in the middle of the night and said she had decided to hang herself. He responded, "Why did you wake me up in the middle of the night when both of us know that you can take your life anytime you choose? Sarah, you don't have the talent for hanging yourself, because you've tried it three times already and broke three ribs." He goes on to say, "Sarah, can you wait til Friday?" "I suppose so," she answered. "Good, then I'll bring sandwiches and we can celebrate your last meal together."

Now, I don't think Olsen was being flippant about suicide. He was trying to get Sarah to see the value of her life and to enjoy what God had given her. As far as I know, she is still around. I believe it is God's Will that we find happiness in THIS lifetime. If we wait until all of our problems disappear before we experience it, we will never find it. Whatever we may think happiness is, it is not the absence of problems or grief and loss. Jesus prayed: "Thy Kingdom come, Thy Will be done, ON EARTH as it is in Heaven."

In the Old Testament, we find this challenge: "Choose this day whom you shall serve...but as for me and my household, we will serve the Lord." (Joshua 24:15)

Life is certainly more than just choosing to live well or being happy despite our circumstances. I want to be happy but I also want to live for a purpose, which is finding God's Will for my life in the here and now. Even in retirement we can make a difference to those around us. It is said that most of us get to Heaven by the way of our hells. This may be true, but I want to experience a little bit of Heaven before I get there. And you know what? I fully believe that I have. Amen.

> Keep your life simple; don't over-schedule and never make a promise you can't keep.

BORN AGAIN PERFUME

I was in a Dallas department store one day and saw this sign over a cosmetic counter: "Born Again Perfume." I didn't buy any, but I've often wondered how it smells. Self-righteous? Humble? It depends.

In John's Gospel, we find the story of Nickodemus, a Pharisee who went to see Jesus one night. He questioned him about the miracles Jesus had performed and in the course of conversation, Jesus told him that he must be born again, if he wanted to enter the Kingdom of God. (John 3:1-6)

This stopped Nick in his tracks. Say what? How can you go back into the womb and start all over? The "new birth" talk didn't make any sense at all. No "born again perfume" for him.

I suspect one reason some people have problems with the church is the message that some give, such as: "you are lost if you don't believe as I believe." There can be a gap between "born-again-talk and born-again-living." People who feel superior because of their beliefs or rituals are prone to start wars. You see it happening, not only in nations, but also in families and churches. I'm allergic to that kind of perfume.

Some talk about "getting saved" because "end-times" are near. People have been predicting the end of the world for a long time. It was supposed to end (as I recall) in 1984, and then in 2000, and 2012. It must be a bit frustrating when it doesn't happen the way they predict. I heard one TV evangelist warn about the coming of Armageddon, but there was still time to send him an offering. Unfortunately, Scripture is sometimes used to "prove" the exact time. There's a statement in Matthew that speaks to this issue: "Heaven and earth shall pass away...but of that day and hour no one knows, not even the angels of heaven...but the Father only" (Mark 13:31-32)

Don't misunderstand me. I'm not knocking being born anew, nor the urgency for doing so. Most, if not ALL of us could change for the better. But I believe when Jesus spoke of the new birth, he was referring to flashes of light in the dark places of our lives. It's like living in a 10-room house. You may turn the light on in one room, but this doesn't mean every room has light. Salvation, according to my finite mind, is a process that's on-going. It's a matter of spiritual growth.

Put it this way: Here is a man who is addicted to a self-destructive habit. The addiction is dangerous, and puts poison in his body. Then, one day, the LIGHT dawns and he realizes that he is on a dead-end street and says: "With God's help, I will beat this thing." And it happens. New birth. New beginning. New outlook on life. Feeling good.

Now, this doesn't mean that a person is suddenly transformed in EVERY way. He may not be a good husband or responsible father or there may be other areas in his life that need light. I know a man who claims to be a born-again Christian, yet he is prejudiced against anyone who is not white, or Protestant. That kind of perfume is rancid.

Being born again means that you are willing to put on better tapes, listen to better directions, and try healthier life-styles. It involves body, mind and spirit.

A personal illustration: Since 1981, I have survived two, not one, but TWO by-pass heart surgeries. I've wondered, "What am doing that's bringing this on?" After the first surgery, I kept hearing "low-fat diet." And I thought I was doing pretty good with that and then WHAM, another "party" in the hospital 2008. I have become convinced (the hard way) that my eating habits need re-evaluating.

The thing that caught my attention was the book *Prevent and Reverse Heart Disease* by Caldwell B. Esselstyn, Jr. M.D. A former surgeon, researcher and clinician, Dr. Esselstyn spent 20 years studying nutrition and convincingly argues that plant-based, oil-free nutrition can not only prevent heart disease, but also reverse its effects. He advises his clients not to eat anything with a "mother" or a "face." The proof is in the number of people with coronary disease who tried it over a number of years. Their cholesterol and heart problems virtually disappeared.

So, I am striving to be a vegetarian, although I have a little trouble passing up shrimp and other seafood.. Speaking of eating things without a face, one sympathetic friend said: "Well, Henry, if you pull the heads off of shrimp, then they have no face." Great point.

I received a birthday card the other day from my oldest son that depicted a woman, talking to her husband: "I agree, eating right and exercising do make you feel younger. But they don't have to make you ACT younger. Now, get rid of that sports car, nose ring and ponytail."

It seems to me that the "new birth" is dynamic, and by nature moves toward holistic living, when the body, mind and spirit are working together. No one has any guarantees about the length of life on planet earth, but it's just plain good sense that we stay as healthy and happy as long as we can. The Bible reminds us that these bodies are holy temples (I Cor. 6-19-20)

Then too, a person who feels good is more apt to enter into a better dialogue with a Loving God, who claims us whether we eat right or not, thank you Lord. But the point is-the Lord may claim us a lot SOONER if we don't take care of ourselves.

HOW CAN WE BE CONTENT IN A WORLD LIKE THIS?

Contentment is hard to come by. Just when I think I'm content, I get a phone call, or see something on TV about a kid being brutalized, or a letter from Smile Train with the picture of a distorted-faced child, and they are begging for donations. This is just a tip of the urgent call to help correct situations that are pitifully wrong.

In the summer of 1934, the famous theologian, Reinhold Niebuhr, was vacationing at his summer cottage near Heath, Massachusetts. As often happened he was invited to conduct the services one Sunday in a small church nearby. At the end of his sermon, he offered this prayer: "O God give us the serenity to accept what cannot be changed, courage to change what should be changed, and wisdom to distinguish the one from the other." At the end of the service, someone asked him for a copy of it, whereby Niebuhr reached into his Bible and got out a crumpled sheet of paper and said: "Here, take this Prayer, I shall have no further use for it."

Niebuhr didn't realize how much impact this prayer would have. The man who received the prayer put it on his Christmas card, and the founder of Alcoholics Anonymous saw it and adopted it as their official motto. The USO picked it up and printed millions of copies during World War II, and even today it is still used by multitudes. Niebuhr may not have sensed any further use for the prayer, but it has become the most loved and most widely known prayer in the world, next to the Lord's Prayer.

Why has this prayer become so powerful? We are, day by day, confronted with two kinds of realities. On the one hand are things we cannot change, those realities that will still be there after we have ranted and raved and condemned. We can say, "Ain't it awful!" all day long and never change a thing. There will always be those things that CAN be changed and ought to be changed. And we need the wisdom to distinguish the one from the other.

This prayer is uniquely Biblical. In the Genesis account of creation, God made the world and right in the middle of creating it, God made man and invited him to participate in the completion of the enterprise. Man's place is right in the middle, as sort of a co-creator, amid that which has already been done and before what was yet to be done. Man is called on to be fruitful, to multiply, "to exercise dominion over the plants and "animals." God gives to humans, males and females, the gift in incompletion. The male and female roles can also apply to the different ways of relating to life.

For example, the male role, in classic terms, has been understood as that of the initiator, the instigator, the one who makes things happen. The female role is that of the responder, the consenter, the one who allows things to happen. In the Christmas story, the angel Gabriel appeared to Mary and told her of the great thing being proposed for her by God. When Mary responded to this by saying, "Let it be to me as Thou has spoken," this is a classic illustration of the feminine role. Now the point of the Genesis account is that both of these roles are needed. One is not superior to the other. But there are times when they need to switch roles. To be ONLY male, that is, always instigating, or ONLY female—always consenting—would be incomplete humanness. This has finally reached our awareness as human beings.

This is exactly what Niebuhr calls for in his prayer. There are times when it is appropriate for every person to act from a feminine role and say, "Let it be to me as it must be. Here is something I cannot change, but I must accept. I consent." And there are times when it is appropriate to act out of the masculine role, and say, "Here is something that we can change. Let us create." It is a wise thing to act out of the male and female roles. Wisdom comes when we realize which role is appropriate. To accept things or to change them—that's the issue.

Paul was acting out of the female role when he wrote to the Philippians 4:11, "I have learned in whatever circumstances I am in, to be content." He knew how to accept the things he couldn't change, and yes—look at the impact of his writings. He brought change wherever he traveled and won people to a new way of thinking. Paul had more problems than you could shake a stick at. The thorn in the flesh gave him fits, but he finally learned how to accept it and move on. He learned how to be content despite his difficulties.

So, if you are faced with tremendous difficulties, illness, ill-will or whatever, stop and ask, "What are my options? What are the things I can do something about? And what are the things I need to accept, by the Grace of God?"

May God help us to accept the things that can't be change, the courage to change the things we can and the wisdom to know the difference. Amen.

LOST IN YOUR OWN BACKYARD

Many of us have heroes, people we would like to emulate and pattern our lives after. Personalities rubs off on us, and without always being aware of it, we are influenced by their behavior. You and I are very contagious when it comes to attitudes and actions. Tell me who your heroes are, and I will introduce you to yourself, because what or who we admire usually becomes part of us.

One of my heroes is the father in the story of the prodigal son found in Luke 15. He welcomed his wayward son home despite the fact that the son had squandered his birthright and fellowshipped with pigs. It's a classic story of grace and forgiveness on the part of the father.

I know parents who try to hold on to their kids, even when they are grown and this produces a lot of dysfunction, and heartache.

There's an old joke about a young man who came in one day and said to his father, "I want the money that I worked for." When asked what he planned to do with it, the son said, "I want to go to Las Vegas, and see the bright lights, and kick up my heels and pass a good time with wine, women and song." The father said, "Son, I just have one request." "What's that, dad?" "Take me with you"

That may contain more truth than poetry. However, this was not the case with the prodigal son's father who forgave unconditionally.

This parable has a powerful message today as much as when Jesus gave it. It says we can get into "heap big trouble" when we have no boundaries, when our value system is weak. Many people live by the philosophy that anything goes. The Ten Commandments are just as appropriate today as they were centuries ago. We have freedom of choice which can be violated. It's good that we are not puppets on a string, but we can stand in our own way, and become our worst enemy.

There's not enough laws to cover all aspects of human behavior. There never will be. Perhaps the greatest law is within ourselves. Unless we have an "inner policeman," a sense of conscience, we can be self-destructive to ourselves and to others. We can hurt people, even the people who brought us into this world, those we love most.

The older brother had done things right. He had stayed home and helped his dad. His problem was a terrible attitude. When he heard about his kid brother wasting his money and his dad giving him a party, he became jealous, angry and full of self-pity. It does seems unfair. His dad was rewarding the wayward son and there he was—without any recognition for his faithfulness. The problem child always gets more attention than the others, fair or not. One son or daughter seems to get "the blessing" from parents, while the other siblings complain about parental favoritism. It's a familiar story.

I think the point Jesus wanted to emphasize was the father's eagerness to forgive, and to compare it to the forgiveness of God.

Sin is not always something physical, such as murder or stealing or adultery. Sin is also a state of mind and emotion, a spiritual condition that separates us from God. It's not just killing, it's anger. It's not just adultery, its lust.

I believe salvation is always specific. What are we saved from? What are we saved for? Some are saved from being an alcoholic. Or a negative attitude or an adulterer. I believe we can get "unsaved" in a hurry by falling back into old habits or attitudes. We call it "falling from grace."

I will close this the story of a woman whose son was killed accidentally. He was a good athlete, honor student and more. One night she dreamed that she could have him back for 5 minutes. Which experience would she choose? Would it be when he was head of his class? Would it be when he was making a touchdown or receiving an award? No, she said, "If I could have him back for a brief time, it would be when he disobeyed her one day and he came in, put his arms around her and asked for forgiveness." She said, "I saw such love in his eyes."

I believe we have fellowship with God, not during the high moments of praise and winning or doing great things. I believe it's when we fall on our knees in humility and ask for forgiveness. This is the God, like the prodigal's father, who waits for us to come home. Amen.

> What others think of you or whatever they say about you is NONE of your business.

ARE YOU OUT OF YOUR MIND?

Strange question, simple answer. We can live "out of the head" instead of the heart or soul. Perhaps the longest journey you will make in your life-time is from your head to your heart. Healthy people have a combination of both.

On a recent TV show, "So you think you can dance," one of the judges told a contestant, "you are dancing out of your head and not your heart." Everyone agreed, even the contestant. The same holds true about musicians as well as many other professions. One of the highest compliments I've received as a minister, is "you really spoke to us out of your heart today," which usually meant that I was preaching to ME. I wonder how many sermons I've preached when my heart wasn't in it.

Singing or dancing or speaking from the heart is soul-full., expressing our deepest feelings. Soul-full living is right brain stuff, like singing, dancing, playing, loving, and creating. The soul helps us to be imaginative, intuitive, and to get in touch with our emotions. When people say: "My gut feeling tells me thus and so," they are coming from the soul.

"As a man thinketh in his heart, so is he." (Proverbs 23:7) We tend to become what we think about, similar to the old adage: "We are what we eat." We can THINK ourselves into a depression or anxiety in no time at all. What we think about produces our feelings. If we change our thoughts, our feelings will change.

This is not to down-play the mind at all. The brain or the mind is a miraculous gift from the Creator God. It helps us to choose, learn, solve problems and so on. But it can be our worst enemy or our best friend. As long as we identify with the mind, we will pollute it with worry, anger, fear and so on. You are more than your mind. You are a spirit.

People who master life refuse to be pushed around by negative thoughts. This is not to hide your head in the sand, but if you listen to the voice in your head exclusively, you may end up judging, comparing, complaining and imagining the worst. The mind can play tricks on you, and play old "tapes" such as "I'll never amount to anything, or "I don't belong," or "I don't have any talent," etc.

Eckhart Tolle, in his book "The Power of Now" says when we listen to our mind "thinking" and realize that here I am listening to it, this "I am" is a sense of your presence that opens the door to reality." I believe that this "I am" is also our connection to God, the Great I am.

Emotions are signals from the soul. Every emotion offers information about you that is important. Our emotions are expressions of the soul. Spiritual growth comes from listening to these emotions with the desire of bringing them in line with your faith in God.

If you try to live exclusively out of your head (left brain), it may keep you from learning to swim, or paint, or play musical instrument or whatever you'd like to do but your mind won't let you take the risk Your mind can sabotage you just by "thinking" you can't do this or that. If you live out of your phobias, life can be just one scary thing after another.

We live in a time when the mind is suffering from information-overload. We are almost forced into head-living by trying to keep up with internets, numbers, systems, charts, gains and losses, and other stress-producing technological advances. Soul-full living, or spiritual growth will just have to wait until we take care of business, which may take too long, if we are not careful.

So, find time to give expression to the needs of your spirit. Take time for soul-full living Get in touch with your dreams. Wake up to the beauty of creation. Find time to meditate and to pray, and feel your connection to all living things.

I believe that the Apostle Paul knew a lot of this soul/mind stuff long ago when he wrote to the Philippians, "Whatever is true, whatever is honorable, whatever is just, whatever is pure, whatever is lovely, whatever is gracious, if there is any excellence, if there is anything worthy of praise, think about these things." (4:8)

In the meantime, keep watch over your mind, not as your master, but your slave. The mind is a great instrument. I wouldn't want to leave home without it.

You have a right to say "no" and you don't have to explain why.

SOME ASSEMBLY REQUIRED

One of the most frustrating Christmas experiences I can remember was when Santa brought a boxed-up toy kitchen set (stove, sink and all) to one of our daughters. We worked almost all Christmas Eve trying to assemble that thing. And then there were a few missing parts left over.

I believe life is like that. God has given us certain "tools and a bag of rules" to assemble to find the best life possible. Jesus said "I have come that you may have life and live it more abundantly." (John 10:10) We need to assemble the right ingredients to make this happen.

Take love for example. The word could mean almost anything today, but in the deepest sense, it means to accept others as we want to be accepted, to treat others the way we want to be treated. This means a lack of control of others, because the only one you can control is yourself. Love means to forgive others even when they don't ask for it. It means seeing beyond labels and types without regard to race, religion or gender. Love is our main part to assemble. The instructions are clear in Scripture: "Love the Lord your God with all your heart, and with all your soul, and with all your strength, and your neighbor as yourself."(Luke 10:28)

There are many levels of love, but look at the way it applies to your family. What kind of "bonding" is in your family? Desmond Tutu once said, "You don't choose your family. They are God's gift to you, as you are to them." So treat them with care.

Good family relationships need to be nourished and protected and strengthened thru the years. Beneath the exterior that all of us have (which the ego creates), there is a needy child that wants to be loved, forgiven and accepted. It's strange how we project certain expectations onto parents, preachers and others—and if they don't live up to our agenda, we tend to write them off. And we miss knowing the person on a deeper level. Also, during illness, suffering and death, if our family is not there for us, who will be?

I heard a psychiatrist say: "When people love each other, they give God to each other. And when they don't give love, they can give each other the devil."

I like the letter a little boy wrote to God: "Dear God, I know you said to love one another, but you don't know my sister." We aren't commanded to "like" everyone but love is a different matter altogether.

In the Gospel according to Luke, a Pharisee invited Jesus for dinner. The Pharisees didn't care for Jesus and I've often wondered why he was invited in the first place. But guess who came to dinner? A woman of the streets. She brought perfume and poured it on Jesus' feet and wept as she wiped them with her hair. It was truly an act of love. When Simon saw it, he said to Jesus: "Do you know WHO this is?" Jesus told him that this was a woman, a human being who had shown great love. This was more than Simon had done. Sin is not always some overt action such as adultery or stealing. Sin is refusing to see or hear the person next to you. It is judging another person because of gender or the color of one's skin. Simon saw a "type"—Jesus saw a human being.

We don't understand God at all unless we understand that God is in all of us. And even if we don't assemble every part in the right way, God is there not to condemn us but to redeem us. Jesus made it plain that he did not come to judge nor to condemn the world.

Now, about that kitchen set we tried to assemble on that Christmas Eve— I'm not sure exactly what happened to it. It probably fell apart in a week or so. But love was still there.

SEX IS A SACRED TRUST

Dr. Billy Graham made this remark in one of his columns: "Sex is a sacred trust, not to be abused." Many agree with this, yet, is there anything being abused more than sex in our culture? Not merely in our country, but the world over. Sex sells everything from horse collars to corn flakes.

I was brought up within a traditional marriage, as most of us were. My folks lived by the admonition in Genesis 2:24 - "A man leaves his father and his mother and cleaves to is wife." My parents remained "cleaved" over fifty years. I am the youngest of six children, so my Dad took seriously that we should "go forth and multiply."

Yet, we all us know that other life-styles exist and have done so for centuries and will probably continue for as long as the Lord only knows. I was also taught not to be quick to be judgmental. Whatever this world is coming to has already come-whether we approve or not. Disapproval of alternate life-styles doesn't change anything, because as Richard Rohr reminds us, we are made up of three parts: one third nature, one third nurture and one third free choice.

I used to get the impression that people became uncomfortable if the preacher started talking about "sex and such" from the pulpit. Somehow, I got the impression that you either had to love God and hate sex or hate God and love sex. Hopefully this is a thing of the past.

This column happens to be my "pulpit," so let's get real. Great sex occurs when sexuality is driven by spirituality. It occurs when the commitment is sincere, and responsible, otherwise it can come across as cheap or vulgar or abusive.

In our older church wedding ceremony, it says, "Marriage is an honorable estate, instituted of God and signifying to us the mystical union which exists between Christ and His church. Which holy estate Christ adorned and beautified with his presence in Cana of Galilee. It is therefore not to be entered into unadvisedly, but reverently, discreetly, and in the fear (respect) of God." It seemed that Jesus loved weddings and celebrated them fully, for he said, "I have come that you may have life and have it abundantly." (See John 2, 1-11 and John 10:10)

Sex sins seem to be the hardest to forgive. A person can abuse his family, lie, cheat and steal and get away with it, but let that person run off with a co-worker, and it's all over. Sometimes, there is no grace or forgiveness at all. This was not true with those who wrote the Bible. To them, sexual sins weren't different from other sins.

And Biblical writers didn't avoid sex. Sins were to be forgiven and learned from. When Jesus talked with the woman at the well with five husbands, he proceeded to talk to her about the true worship of God. (John 4:16-26) Or consider David's adultery, or Rahab the harlot, or Hosea's wife who sold herself into prostitution, or the woman caught in adultery and Jesus asking her to "Go, and sin no more." It seems that every one of them recovered.

Sex connects us with our own creativity. Thus, we become co-creators with God. This makes it sacred. Our sexuality is the "God-likeness" in us. (Read Genesis 1 and 2). God saw all of creation as "good."

If the definition of marriage comes from the law-givers or the government, we can become very confused and frustrated, especially if it conflicts with religious concepts and beliefs. A piece of legal paper doesn't make a marriage. The legal part satisfies the state laws and protects the spouse, children, property, etc. The glue that holds a relationship together is commitment, responsibility, love, and not a piece of paper.

Evidently, people can meet their needs outside of traditional marriage. Again, whether I agree with it or not makes little difference. I have to make my own choices, and live by them. Getting upset over same-sex liaisons is like condemning the grass because it's green. It just is, that's all. This goes back to days of Plato and beyond.

"Giving civil rights to people who are responsible citizens need not be an issue," said one of the TV commentators. We live in a culture that is over-mothered and under-fathered. If a boy has two mothers, he is likely to be molded into the mother's image of what a boy or a man should be. If a child has two fathers, one of them had better be nurturing and motherly, or there will be problems. This gets complicated, right?

Labels don't do it for me. Labels separate people and keep people from knowing and appreciating those who are different. If we are going to be a community, we must see beyond labels and categories and find human beings who struggle just like everyone else. Respect for each other is the key to a solid community. Prejudice in various forms keeps tearing communities down.

The other evening when I was watching Anderson Cooper on TV, they showed a report on Syria, and I was almost traumatized by the bloody scenes of a nation being destroyed by its own leader, and then we saw the thousands being murdered in Mexico by drug cartels. Then, Anderson talked about other crises in the world, and during the middle of his broadcast, I thought about the hatred that exists in our country toward people who are different. The marriage issue seems almost trite by comparison.

Enough serious stuff. It's time for a smile.

My spouse and I were standing in a ticket line to go to a function. I reached for my wallet only to discover very little cash. I turned to her and asked her if she had any money. "I didn't bring my purse," she answered.

I said to the lady behind the ticket counter (laughingly): "I may have to get rid of this woman."

The ticket lady looked up and said dryly: "Sir, you'd better hold on to her, 'cause not many more trains are going to pull into your station."

IT'S YOUR FAMILY—FOR
BETTER OR WORSE

She was dead serious when she said to me, "Just because we both came from the same birth mother doesn't mean that we have to be close." She and her sister had not spoken to each other for years. I listened to her, and I felt a little sad that two sisters quit trying to have a good relationship and settled for bitter feelings.

If you have a close family, you are among the very blessed on earth. Nothing else even comes close. When holidays come around, many families get together and will have a chance to renew family ties and enjoy being together. Some dread it like the plague and will go through the motions, but they can hardly wait until it's over.

Families are scattered to the four corners today. Our mobility has devalued the role of the grandparents, but many studies indicate that being near family is one of the most highly desired elements of retired persons. In fact, various research indicates that people who retain close family relationships live longer and are more functional.

Grandparents are important to children. They (we) have a special role in helping to shape their lifestyle and faith.

The image of grandparents has changed through the years. One of my grandmothers looked like a little dried-up prune, and died at age 71. Today's grandmother is attractive, slender, stylish and drives a convertible all over town. Many have high-paying jobs as executives and CEOs.

Faith tends to run in the family. The Apostle Paul wrote to his protégé Timothy: "I am reminded of your sincere faith, a faith that dwelt in your grandmother, Lois, and, I am sure, dwells in you." (II Tim.5) The example of one generation can influence several generations. It's like the relay race I saw the other evening watching the Olympics. One person passes the baton on to the other. The role of grandparents can become the second line of defense against some of the issues facing young people today.

I've been a grandfather a long time, and I think I've learned a few things. Let me share them with you.

First, I need to be careful about giving advice to parents, unless it's asked for. Even if I disagree with the way a grandchild is being raised, I need to go easy with my "great" wisdom in raising kids. No doubt I made as many errors as anyone else at this point.

I've also learned not to tell my children and grandchildren all my aches and pains. A friend said to me recently: "Every time I go to see my Mother, she rehearses all of her arthritis pains and everything else that's wrong, and I am reaching the point where I dread going to see her." Our children need to know when we are seriously ill but let's spare them otherwise.

I need to remember to send my "grands and greats" birthday cards and remember other events but I need to be careful with gifts. It's easy to over-indulge grandchildren.

Don't be preachy, but talk about your own faith to your grandchildren. As they grow older, and encounter difficult situations, they will draw strength from your experience.

I officiated at a funeral for a woman in Lake Charles, and the thing that made it a beautiful service was what one of her grandchildren said about her. She gave me a copy, and I will quote it:

"Grandmother, you had a way of healing all of us with skinned knees and wounded hearts in the rocking chair. When we misbehaved, you said it was nothing more than missing a nap. Through you, we gained an appreciation for morning because we woke up at your house to the smell of fresh biscuits, bran muffins, and strong coffee. You started the day with, "Good morning, sunshine!" and left lipstick on our cheeks.

"You made us feel important by taking us with you on your mail route. You played games with us and taught us how to play fair and not cheat. You taught us the importance of doing chores out of love, and not just for money. You attended our dance and piano recitals and sporting events. You were always proud of us even when we made mistakes. You taught us how to cook and we remember your pies and cakes.

"You gave us a sense of spirituality, an understanding of responsibility and an awareness of good manners. You gave us an appreciation of art, and took 6 mischievous children and turned us into young ladies and gentlemen.

"You taught us to love God, respect our parents, and certainly to make our beds when we were guests in someone else's home.

"For all these things we are grateful. Your values are part of our lives.

"We love you very much, signed 6 grandchildren."

I DO WINDOWS

In the Apostle Paul's letter to the Corinthians, he wrote, "Now we see in a glass darkly, but then face to face. Now I know in part, but then I shall understand fully, even as I have been fully understood." (I Corinthians 13:12)

The city of Corinth was well known for the production of mirrors or glass, made of polished metal. But, apparently, they did not reflect a clear image.

Is this the way it is with our understanding of God's Way and Will? There are times when we are puzzled about life's mysteries. We are frustrated by life's hurtful experiences, and we lack a clear understanding. If God is all-loving, why goes God permit certain things to happen? If God is all-powerful, why does God allow it?

We are told that God is love, but there are occasions when we walk to the edge of our faith searching for answers. Where is God in all of this? Where is love?

According to one psychologist, when people reach 60 or 70, they become bitter or sweeter. We don't have to reach 60 for this to happen. We grow sweeter or bitter as the years come and go.

In every bad situation, there is hope and redemption.

I must get rid of self-pity, first of all. It is so easy to let this disease of the spirit take over and rob us of wholeness and happiness. It can cripple the strongest among us if we allow it.

A boy dropped out of high school and joined the Navy. He explained his plight: "The teachers were always picking on me." It's easy to blame others for what we do or don't do. "The world is picking on me, so I will... (Whatever)." Some lick their wounds from childhood and never get beyond them.

Our hope is also found in the act of forgiveness. We need to begin by forgiving ourselves. A sense of guilt can be crippling. We see through a glass darkly because our spiritual windows are dirty. We have blurred vision because of greed or jealousy or prejudice. One of the hymns we sing in church has these lines: "He (God) breaks the power of cancelled sin; he sets the prisoner free." (Charles Wesley, Methodist Hymnal 157) I don't want to go through life imprisoned by guilt.

We live in an unusual time in history. I've never witnessed such pessimism and negativism about our country and our future. Bad news drip from every newscast. There is disillusionment all around us, and it's hard not to feel depressed. Sometimes I feel that I need to DO something quickly, but I'm not sure what to do. It's like someone has dumped problems in my lap that I don't know how to solve. No wonder people are stressed out.

This is when it becomes necessary to call on my faith. I need to believe that this is still God's world and NOTHING can separate us from God's love.

A friend shared this experience with me recently. She said that her son was killed in an accident a few years ago, and it affected her vision. Everything was hazy and dim and there seemed to be frost on every window. She went to church and heard a sermon on the Resurrection, and the words went straight to her heart. She finally heard a hopeful sound. According to her, the dimness has lifted and the frost has disappeared.

Thank God there's hope. It has been said that HOPE is frosting on the cake. I believe it is the cake itself. "Now we see in a glass darkly, but then face to face." (I Cor. 13:12)

Listen real close, and you may hear the whisper of the Small, Still Voice: "I do windows."

A CASE FOR COMPASSION

Despite the disorder and violence in our world today, compassion is still at work in wonderful ways.

The following incident came from a newspaper in Japan.

In order to renovate a house, its occupants tore down the wall. Japanese houses usually have a hollow space between the wooden walls. While demolishing the house, the owner found a lizard that had been nailed to the wall through one foot. When he saw this, felt compassion and curiosity. After researching it, he learned that the house was two years old, and evidently the lizard had been there ever since.

It seemed unbelievable that a live creature could "hang on" for two years in one position. As the facts unfolded the man laid the partition aside to observe how the lizard had survived without moving at all.

This is what the owner discovered. Another lizard appeared with food in its mouth and gave it to his mate, thus keeping it alive for two years. Imagine.

I was moved when I read this story and I thought about the relationships between family members, friends, lovers and siblings. Sometimes we let people slip out of our lives without expressing much thoughtfulness or thankfulness.

When we visit a cemetery, we wish we had done or said more while they were still with us. If such compassion can happen to one of God's tiny creatures, like lizards, think about the possibilities on a human level.

There are times, to be sure, when all of us may feel "nailed to the wall." How we need to be here for each other. The blessings of a kind word, a warm greeting, a helping hand, can be poetry to the heart and music to the soul.

The words from the 43rd chapter of Isaiah comes to mind:

"Do not be afraid, for I have redeemed you; I have called you by name. You are mine. When you pass through the waters, I will be with you, and through the rivers, they shall not overwhelm you. When you walk through the fire you shall not be burned and the flames shall not consume you. For I am the Lord your God, the Holy One of Israel, the Saviour."

THE "YIN AND YANG"
OF OUR FAITH

"One day, I'm up, one day, I'm down, yes, Lord, yes." Or so goes an old spiritual, "Nobody knows the trouble I've seen ..." (Methodist Hymnal, pg.520, WF Smith)

You've probably noticed by now that faith doesn't stand still. There is an ebb and flow, yin and yang, a "sometimes I'm up and sometimes I'm down" to the faith dimension that many experience.

We see this in Jesus' disciples. They were combinations of contradictions, and inconsistencies to say the least. There is a verse in Matthew: "They saw him; some worshipped and some doubted." Some drew close and some backed away. If nothing else we see the ebb and flow of faith as they go to one side and then another. We see this also in the Psalms. "My soul bowed down to the dust." (Psalm 44) Or consider the words of Jesus on the cross: "My God, my God, why have you forsaken me?"

What we believe in is so important that almost everything else depends on it. Beliefs determine actions. Faith is taking the next step, not knowing exactly where it will lead. Faith is believing in the goodness of life, although we don't always see it. Faith is believing in the ultimate triumph of good over evil. Faith can be more adequately felt than defined.

Our lives will likely never be free from turmoil and testing. There will be stress and tension and all manner of heartache. The only area that is strictly up to me is my personal faith. I can accept God's forgiveness and live within God's Grace, or pass it by.

Faith is staring at the hospital ceiling after being told its malignant, and not being afraid. Faith is losing someone by death or divorce but believing God will help you to move on. Faith becomes the opposite of religion; it is not anxious to please God nor to prove God's existence. Faith simply serves God out of trust, and builds a life on the greatness of God's love.

The evolution of the species is not a threat to me at all. All we have to do is to look around and we see the ongoing of creation as trees grow as well as babies and other beings. God refuses to be static or fixed. We worship a dynamic God who will not be confined to anyone's particular idol, symbol, doctrine or institution.

It is said that "right-brain" people find faith much easier than the "left-brainers." Left-brain folks seem to be more analytical, factual, calculating, scientific, and exacting: while right-brain people are more intuitive, sentimental, feeling, musical, artistic, emotional and imaginative. Left-brainers want to put everything to the test, deduce facts, and may have a hard time trying to fathom the great spiritual truths. Right-brainers seem to experience faith at a deeper level. They know you can't put faith in a test-tube. Either side can be strengthened by choice.

It's okay to doubt. Perhaps this is the only way we can have a faith of our own.

I believe God is in our YIN as well as in our YANG. Consider these words from Psalm 139: "Where shall I go from Your Spirit? Or where shall I flee from Your presence? If I make my bed in hell, behold, You art there. If I take the wings of the morning, and dwell in the uttermost parts of the sea; even there shall Your hand lead me, and Your right hand shall hold me."

I love the story of Jonah being swallowed by a tight-lipped whale. The author of this story is making this point: We cannot eclipse the presence of God, even in the belly of a whale. God is with us, period.

So, whether our faith ebbs or flows, we need to celebrate it. The more we celebrate it the stronger it becomes.

Erma Bombeck tells about a little boy in church, not bothering anyone, but every now and then, he would turn around and smile at her. He did this several time when suddenly his mother jerked him around and told him to stop that grinning, that he was in church. Tears came to boy's eyes as he turned around. Erma said: "I wanted to get up and give that boy a big hug and tell him about a happy, smiling God."

May God help us to celebrate our faith in all of our ebbing and flowing. I don't know who penned these words, but they speak to me:

"My life is but a weaving
Between my God and me,
Sometimes he weaveth sorrow
And I in foolish pride
Forget he sees the upper and
I—the underside."
Amen.

THE DESTRUCTIVE POWER
OF JUDGING

Judgmentalism and fault-finding seems to be a favorite indoor sport. If someone doesn't pass our "virtue" test, we can cross them off our list. One of the most important Biblical statements in found in Matthew 7:1-2, "Judge not, that you be not judged. For with what judgment you judge, you shall be judged."

Of course, there is a type of criticism and faultfinding that is healthy and essential to our growth. The church, our political structure, our schools and so on will always be in need of constructive criticism.

But there is a spirit of judgmentalism that tears down rather than building up. It condemns rather than commends. It puts people down, especially people who have different religious or political views. The ability to bless or curse each other is powerful indeed, and is more destructive than we realize.

We see this especially during election time. I've never understood why candidates attack each other instead of sticking to their own platform. Every word spoken by the "other" party is scrutinized, dissected and cross-examined. It gets to be a witch hunt rather than an election campaign. And there are certain newscasters and journalists who get nasty with their name-calling. Liberals and conservatives seem to be polarized like never before. It doesn't have to be that way.

I have a minister friend who said he sometimes feels like the congregation is judging him similar to those who judge a gymnastic performance, holding up cards containing the score-like 7.5 for the introduction, 6.9 for the content, and 8.8 for the funny story at the end.

It has occurred to me that being judgmental is one reason more and more people are claiming to be "spiritual, but not religious." Old fundamental concepts of a jealous, vindictive and punishing God is not consistent with God's grace and unconditional love. "Hellfire and damnation preaching" is largely a thing of the past, thank goodness. But let us not resort to "cheap Grace," where we think anything we do or say is okay as long as we ask for forgiveness. Like the farmer who said to his priest, "Father, I want to confess stealing a half load of hay, but I want to be forgiven for stealing the whole load, because I'm going back for the other half tomorrow tonight." Cheap Grace.

Many have left organized religion and are seeking a personal relationship with God akin to the enlightenment of the great Zen masters and Hindu Yogas. This has resulted in a religious cross-pollination where people are thinking for themselves and carving a spiritual lifestyle that may or may not include traditional patterns of worship. Many people are embracing meditation, yoga and other attempts to discover the mystical path to God or to the Self beyond self. (Eckhart Tolle's book *The Power of Now* discusses this subject at length.) Critics call this "new age thinking" and quickly label it as heresy. I think it's a good thing, and makes for a healthier religion.

Matthew Fox has a book, *Original Blessing*, in which he claims that the world was blessed from the beginning, not cursed. This has given rise to a movement called "creation spirituality." It rejects the fallen nature of human beings based on the disobedience of Adam and Eve in the Garden of Eden.

While this may be a positive approach to the Gospel, my main concern is that it seems to negate the power of sin or evil in a person's life. Whether we start with a blessing or a curse, the reality of sin is part of the canvas on which we must live our lives. "While we were yet sinners, Christ died for us," is a major Gospel statement. We don't need God's Grace if we aren't sinful.

So, it seems to me that Christianity could use a good dose of the Eastern practices of meditation, yoga, tai chi, and other techniques, but there comes a time when we must stop gazing at our navels and look for ways to help our neighbors. If you take social action and mission outreach out of Christianity, about all you have left is a narcissistic and self-absorbed system.

Thomas Merton is one of my heroes of the faith. He wrote many books on the art of contemplation. He is famous for the ability to blend his mysticism with social action. He meditated but he also spoke out against the war, and other evils.

So let's stop judging each other and listen to what each has to offer. Let us be open to God's truth, whether we find it in the East or West. Let us pray, not only for our own nation but for the world situation, remembering that we cannot really love God, according to Jesus, unless we love each other.

Judge not, that you be not judged.

HYPOCRITES IN
THE CHURCH? NO WAY

Do you mean there are hypocrites in church on any given Sunday? You gotta be kidding!!

Do you mean that some people never darken the doors of a church or synagogue until they are carried in by 8 pallbearers? Heavens!!

Now let's get serious. One of the things happening today is the number of folks who rebel against organized religion, and they are carving out their own style of worship in non-church settings. Actually, that's not a bad thing. God has never been confined to religious structures. Sure, I can pray on a golf course, or sing the doxology in a fishing boat. But I don't usually do that-although my golfing and fishing could use a little help.

No, I guess the thing I'm talking about is the number of people who say they believe in God or some "higher power," but somewhere along the way 'wrote' the church and synagogue off because they got disillusioned with God's people.

"When I was a child, I was made to go to Sunday school and church every Sunday, and I've had ENOUGH church to last me for a long time," is a common refrain. In too many cases however, believers in exile have every reason to feel this way. They've been hurt by God's people and the sad thing is that when church people say or do hurtful things, you feel that God did it.

The church has always been made up of sinners and saints, hypocrites and holier-than-thous. And when I consider my own "imperfections" (sounds better than "sins"), I realize that I'm right at home with hypocrites. None of us are everything we ought to be. So being sinners is one of the things we have in common.

Maybe we've got the church all wrong. Is it a museum for saints instead of a hospital for sinners? Is it the place we go because we feel we've got it just right and want to show it off? Jesus put it this way: "Those who are well don't need a physician, but those who are sick do" (Matthew 9:12). Is anyone completely well?

So, are you looking for a perfect church, with saints on every pew? Friend, there ain't none, believe me. Okay, so the preacher can't preach, the choir can't sing, and the ushers don't "ush" right. They may need a few prayers and encouragement to do the best they can. Did I join the church to worship the preacher or priest or rabbi? I don't think so.

I rather enjoy looking a little "holy" under a black robe and a white stole, but no one knows better than me that underneath all that religious garb is a scrawny, struggling pilgrim on a journey.

More people attend some type of worship service each week than those attending all sports events combined. Maybe folks want to hear something relevant that could help them to cope better with life. Maybe all of us would be a little less neurotic if we could blend our hearts and voices in corporate worship. Better still, all of us need to reach out with ministries and missions to help heal a hurting and hungry world.

As I look at many decades of ministry within organized religion, I have had a lover's quarrel with the "system" many times, but I can truthfully say that these faulty church people have helped me survive many life changes. Bona fide sinners have ministered to me in times of grief and despair. So I feel right at home with these hypocrites, because I suspect I "R" one.

As the poet says:

There is good in the worst of us
Bad in the best of us,
So it behooves the rest of us,
Not to judge any of us.

And when I realize that organized religion is responsible for helping millions across our globe who suffer from hunger and other maladies, I get a clearer picture of what we are here for.

And when I join other sinners praying, "Thy will be done on earth as it is in Heaven," I believe that it's a good thing to work in that direction.

Looking for a church home? Come join the rest of us hypocrites.

> Stop trying to please everybody, which is impossible anyway.

GRACE IS MORE THAN
A BLUE-EYED BLONDE

Author R. Lofton Hudson tells about a conversation he had with a friend. "What do you think of when I say the word 'Grace?'" The friend smiled and said, "Grace is a blue-eyed blonde." His friend was probably serious because there are many Graces who are blue-eyed and blonde.

But Hudson went on to write a book: "Grace is NOT a blue-eyed blonde." He defines Grace in theological language: "Grace is the unconditional offering of God's love."

We need this kind of love in the world today. The kind that says: "I love you, no matter what." Grace is the prodigal son's father running out to meet the wayward son, not only forgiving him but having a celebration that the son came home. Grace is a husband and wife saying, "I'm sorry," or, "I was wrong," and overlooking each other's faults.

Every relationship needs an abundance of Grace. The Apostle Paul had a thorn in the flesh. We don't know exactly what it was. According to Scripture, he prayed several times that it be taken away, but instead he found the Grace of God to be sufficient.

All of us have thorns in the flesh of one kind or another. I saw a bumper sticker with these words: "God bless this lousy car." There are times when all of us feel lousy. We pray that the thorns be removed, but they are still with us. God doesn't take them away but gives us strength, and patience to deal with them. God is not some kind of cosmic nursemaid to take away all of our problems. God gives us the power we need to cope with our difficulties "Grace-fully."

Sometimes, Grace is with us when we least expect it. It comes in the form of a friend calling another friend to say, "Hello, and how are you?" It comes when we feel forgiven for something stupid. It appears with every kindness we express to another human being.

Grace helps us to love the unlovely and unlovable. It's easy to love people when they love you back. No problem. But try to express unselfish love to a difficult person. Grace can work wonders.

It is said that domestic animals, especially dogs, have lots of Grace. They love you unconditionally. Like the little boy who found a dog by the side of the road. Mangy, dirty, smelly-the dog had been thrown away. The boy begged his father to let him take the dog home. 'Why would you want an animal like that?" the father asked. "Because he wags his tail so good," was the boy's response. He took him home.

Grace reaches beyond party, politics, class, category, color and creed. It says, "I accept you as you are."

I read the other day that one of the reasons the Titanic hit an iceberg and went down was that the radios on the ship were completely jammed with trivial conversation of passengers with friends back home. Other ships in the area could not get through with warning signals. Maybe the reason God's Grace can't get through to us is that our circuits are jammed. We are so busy talking and doing, that we don't have much time to listen, to meditate and to receive what God offers. Grace helps us to stay in tune.

There's an old story about a man who died and was met by St. Peter at the gate of Heaven. "Before I let you in, you need to have earned a thousand points," said Peter.

"Well, uh, I went to church regularly."

"That's 20 points," Peter assured him.

"I gave ten percent of my income to charity," said the man.

"Good, that's 20 more points."

"I took an active part in the community."

"Excellent, that's 20 points."

"Uh, uh, I was good to my family."

"Wonderful, that's 50 points."

The man went on to name every good deed he could remember when he was a Boy Scout and in other activities, earning him 100 more points. Finally, he said, "I can't think of anything else. Goodness, that's only 210 points.

The only way I can get into Heaven is by the Grace of God."

"That's right," said Peter, "Come on in."

> God loves you because of who God is, not because of anything you did or didn't do.

DON'T LOSE YOUR JOY

To a large degree, we decide what we will experience in life and how much joy we will celebrate along the way. Therefore, we need not be satisfied with a few meager crumbs from the table of life—we can go to the party and have a great time.

In this pain-oriented society, we may have to unlearn some things in order to relearn others.

I believe each person is naturally creative. That is, we create the life we live, and the body we will live in. It can be sickly or healthy, energetic or lazy, vibrant or dull. Of course, our bodies and minds are vulnerable to illnesses beyond our control. Yet, even then we choose our response.

There is nothing weird or mysterious about this. Our thoughts have wings that can take us into the most exciting places of the mind. The mind is the BUILDER, and is the universe in miniature.

God is infinite abundance. God has given us the Spirit of truth to guide us so that we may realize and experience every good thing.

I believe many people die not of the aging process, but of utter despair from painful deterioration diseases which reduce pleasure and undermine seeing, hearing, feeling, socializing, and the high level of joy in daily life.

I don't believe we can really know what life is or what joy is, until we experience God. Pleasures come and go, but joy is deep and abiding.

Many live on the circumference of life. That is, we live on the external demands, schedules, and expectations. We are too willing to accept the agenda our society gives us. Rush, rush, rush.

We need to go to the "center," the real essence of life and joy, where everything is stripped away (material things) to find that peace that passes understanding. We cannot really know inner peace and joy until we make peace with our Creator. Most of us experience God during the second half of life, when we begin to lose friends and loved ones, meeting reality head-on.

So, let us be reminded once again that God became fully human in the person of Jesus of Nazareth. God shares our joys as well as our sorrows; our valleys as well as our mountaintop experiences.

"The Word became flesh and dwells among us." (John 1:1) That's worth celebrating.

THE ROAD LESS GRAVELED

Traveling through Arkansas recently, we stopped at a roadside gift shop, and bought a little book of red-neck poems and prose entitled *The Road Less Graveled*, a takeoff on the lines of Robert Frost's famous poem "The Road Not Taken":

> "Two roads diverged in a wood, and I—
> I took the one less traveled by,
> And that made all the difference."

The line, "the one less traveled by," gave birth to the title of Scott Peck's insightful classic, *The Road Less Traveled*, in which he defines love as "the concern you have for the other person's spiritual growth."

There ARE roads less traveled or graveled, for that matter. Roads that the majority may overlook or avoid.Roads that are traveled by those who refuse to conform to the crowd because it may be popular to do so.Roads for those who refuse to be "boxed in" by UNHEALTHY religious belief-systems.Roads that are there for those who seek the truth about life, ultimate realities, and God, who refuse to settle for easy answers or narrow fundamentalism.

Humanity is experiencing unprecedented change today in almost every area of life: technological, ecological, religious, social and political. We now have the ability to manipulate life at the earliest level through genes, cells, organs, tissues, etc. The age of biology is causing us to redefine WHO we are and WHAT we should do on this planet.

Will we play God, and pretend that we have an edge on those who do not believe as we do, or will be begin to see how necessary it is for each of us, regardless of our race, creed, or belief-system, *to understand each other and to realize that we are all interconnected as one family under God?*

The road less traveled is beckoning for those who wish to discontinue the path of self-destruction, and the destruction of others because of religious prejudices.

My point is this: The time is overdue for us to realize that "peace on earth" is not just a pipe dream. It is a necessity for survival! We MUST learn how to live and to help live, or we will face the bumpiest road we have ever traveled.

The major world religions were founded in an early phase of human evolution by those who were ahead of their time, so to speak. They left behind great teachings that hold within them profound seeds of truth about life, relationships and God. But the structures that built up around those religions (including Christianity) have weakened them and undermined their lofty purposes. We have too much bureaucracy and WAY too much hierarchy. We get bogged down in erecting and maintaining buildings and fail to see the importance of the individual. If we ever get beyond the notion that our approach is the only way to God, there is hope.

Now, let me close on a lighter note:

Someone gave me a "tongue in cheek" article that stuck in the back of my mind.

"Who said paved roads was progress? What's mainly wrong with society today is too many dirt roads have been paved. There's not a problem today: crime, drugs, divorce, war, that wouldn't be remedied if we just had more dirt roads.

"Dirt roads give character. People who live at the end of dirt roads learn early on that life is a bumpy ride that it can jar you right down to your teeth sometime, but it is worth it, if at the end is home, a loving spouse, happy kids and a dog.

"There was less crime in the streets before they were paved. Criminals didn't walk dusty miles to rob or rape, if they knew they'd be welcomed by barking dogs and a double-barrel shotgun. And there were no drive-by shootings.

"Our values were better when our roads were worse. People didn't worship their cars more than their kids, and motorists were more courteous and they didn't tailgate by riding the bumper, or the guy in front would choke you with dust and bust your windshield with rocks.

"Dirt roads taught patience. They were environmentally friendly. You didn't hop in your car for a quart of milk or a loaf of bread. You went to the store once a week so there was less car fumes. You walked to the mailbox.

"What if it rained and the dirt road got washed out? That was the best part. You stayed at home and enjoyed some family time, roasted peanuts and popped popcorn. And you learned how to make prettier quilts than anybody.

"At the end of dirt roads ... (HOME)... you soon learned that bad words tasted like soap. Most paved roads lead to trouble. Dirt roads more likely led to the fishing creek, or the swimming hole.

"At the end of a dirt road, there was always extra springtime-income from city dudes who got stuck in the mud, and you'd hitch up a team and pull them out. And you usually got a dollar or more, but you always made a new friend - at the end of a dirt road." (Anon)

LOVE LIKE YOU'VE NEVER
BEEN HURT

There were three frogs on a pad. One decided to jump. How many were left? Three, because you see, he only DECIDED to jump, but he never left the pad.

When it comes to loving another person unconditionally, without expecting anything in return, some may decide it's a good thing, but never make the leap.

Maybe it's because when you love that way, you may get hurt. It's easier to stay with the kind of love that says: "If you don't meet my expectations, we are through." Unconditional love that says, "I will love you, no matter what," can be scary. You risk a broken heart.

This "love principle" is also common in friendships. Broken friendships say, "If you don't play by my rules, hit the road." A lot of friendships are dissolved that way. Someone said if you have 6 or 7 friends who will stay your friend to the very end, NO MATTER WHAT, you are blessed indeed.

Unless you can accept the shortcomings, warts and all, of your spouse, friends, children, whoever, you will be living with disappointment and frustration much of the time. Maybe we need to lower our expectation level. Now, this doesn't mean that you have to live with abuse. You may have to love a person from a distance. It's possible to love a person you don't especially like. Difficult? Yes.

St. Paul in the New Testament says, "Love endures all things." That's always challenged me because I believe some things are unbearable. Was Paul being too idealistic? Maybe so, but let's not give up on our ideals. It may also be unrealistic to think that you can pray for your enemies or go the second mile, as Jesus recommended. But these can be worthwhile goals. Maybe some of us give up on our ideals too easily, and go back to the idea of "an eye for an eye and a tooth for a tooth." That's where much of humanity has been for a long time, nations included.

Unselfish love can change the lover as well as the loved. Conventional wisdom has it that when it comes to change, you can only change yourself. I'm not at all sure about that. I believe you CAN love a person into changing. The loved one will WANT to change under love's power to keep from hurting the lover. It may not always happen, but it's sure worth a try. I've seen unconditional love at work and although it leaves the heart exposed, it's worth every ounce of forgiveness, patience and understanding.

After the tragic earthquake in Haiti, I overheard someone say, "If God loves us, why do such horrible things happen?" Is this a fair question? Human beings have always been vulnerable to natural disasters that have no conscience. It's the kind of world we live in. Why do we blame God for such tragedies? It also seems to me that God offers us love in our darkest moments, a love that knows no boundaries. I believe God is at work through doctors and nurses and so many people who are reaching out to the people of Haiti in one way or the other. When love reaches out, God is there, and we certainly see it now. God's amazing grace is expressed through people. Nothing has ever insured us against the hurt from natural disasters.

One other thing: We need to quit trying to please God for the wrong reasons. Let's stop looking upon God as one who rewards our good deeds and punishes the bad ones. This makes us neurotic because we cannot know how much "pleasing" it takes to satisfy God. And if we only love God out of fear of punishment, or trying to get to Heaven, we've missed the whole meaning of God's Grace. We love God to create a relationship. Love has intrinsic value.

So, if you've been hurt by any kind of love or by the circumstances of life (and who hasn't?) don't let resentment or self-pity dominate your life. Let us not be "human frogs" and stay on our pads because we are afraid getting hurt.

Believe me, there' a much better way.

Some people had rather be right than to have a good marriage.

IS DEATH A DIRTY JOKE?

It would be utter arrogance for me to write about death as if I knew a great deal more about it than you. I know that it happens, and, in many cases, much too quickly, according to my judgment. Although we read about individuals who have had "out of body" experiences or "after death and back to life" images, it's easy to be skeptical about such reports. On the other hand, it's hard to argue with first-hand experience.

It was an atheist who said that "death is just a dirty joke for those who are unlucky enough to be born." WHOA, wait just a minute, how dismal. I would respond by saying that the atheist expresses an opinion based on ignorance also.

Many fear death because it remains unknown territory despite the reports of those who have claimed they've been there and back. It is easy to spout off a few platitudes and console ourselves with a few nice words but it takes more than words for me. I need a strong faith that gives me an assurance and a peace about dying, and a firm hope about being with loved ones beyond this life. When so many loved ones are on the "other side," I must find a way to believe that God is on both sides of the grave.

I am in the Judeo-Christian tradition, which is an enormous support system for my faith. There is real comfort in these words: "Though I walk through the valley of the shadow of death, I will fear no evil, for Thou art with me." (Ps. 23) And I cannot ignore the words of Jesus in John 14, or Paul's counsel in I Corinthians 15.

The Scriptures tell me also that the very hairs of my head (there aren't many left) are numbered. This is fantastic, almost irrational, and yet it points to the faith in a Higher Being who cares about the minutia of each human being. It implies that we are important, precisely because God gave us that importance via creation.

Although a mystery, death, it seems to me, is not the end of who we are. We are not dissolved in the phenomenon of death as the drop of water dissolves into the ink well. I believe there is a continuum between the uniqueness of our biography created in our years here and in the distant past. We have received through our genes the whole heritage of the human race. How, for instance, when you were born, did you know to feed upon your mother's breast? It is instinct—you didn't do it; no experience gave it to you, and you don't even remember doing it.

Or let me put it this way: A part of you was extended before your birth into the genetic stock of your parents. You contribute to that stockpile during your lifetime, and this continues into subsequent generations. Death, then, must be a continuation of this kind of evolution, it seems to me. Eventually your body is cast aside, no longer useful. Your spirit, or soul, or the center of your being, survives because of this constant progression. Of course, our finite minds cannot comprehend the form it takes, and it's not up to us to figure it out. It's not our show, for all of it is wrapped up in a faith that reaches from this world to the next.

I was talking with a young friend last week who said he believes in reincarnation, the return of the spirit into another human body. This opens up a whole new can of worms. Frankly I just hope I make it during THIS lifetime, but as he put it, "If I can't get it right this time, maybe I'll make it in the next go-around."

"SWEET ARE THE USES
OF ADVERSITY"

The one-liner above is from Shakespeare's *As You Like It*. I am fascinated by clichés, one-liners and old sayings. Especially the ones that have been around a long time, and no one seems to know their origin.

My parents used a lot old sayings that I use to this day, such as, "He looks like death warmed over," or, "We have enough food to feed Cox's army." (Who was Cox?) My former mother-in-law had a saying that blew me away: "He looks like death eating a cracker?" She gave this explanation: "Years ago when people died at home, the last image of them in bed was sipping a little broth with a cracker." Makes sense to me.

"Don't let it get your goat" is a familiar cliché that, according to my source, began when race horse owners put a goat in the stable of their horse the night before the big race. The presence of the placid goat would calm the horse so he would be more relaxed for the race. And sometimes, an un-scrupulous gambler would steal the goat, knowing his competitor's horse wouldn't run as well. Whatever the origin, life does have a way of getting our goat at times, especially when we feel defeated, frustrated or having lost control.

Shakespeare nailed it when he said, "Sweet are the uses of adversity." I've seen people take the most "gosh-awful" circumstances and they seem to find inner peace despite everything. They live ABOVE their circumstances rather than UNDER them. They find something positive in the negatives.

The Scriptures are full of both examples. David, in the Old Testament, had more problems than he could handle, most of them self-made. His son Absolom rebelled, and one day David said, "If I had the wings of a dove, I would fly away and be at rest." We see another side of David in the Psalms. For example, look at these words from Psalm 37:1-4, 7: "Do not fret because of the wicked and do not be envious of wrong doers, for they will soon fade like the grass and wither like the green herb... Take delight in the Lord... Be still before the Lord and wait patiently for Him."

I think it would be almost impossible to go through life without fretting about different things. But complaining demands a lot of time and energy and rarely solves anything. People who are constant "fretters" can easily become sociopathic. Some go off the deep end, hating the government and everything authoritative, thinking nothing is right and then something may snap and they are moved to kill others at random. This is anger losing control. This form of "mental illness" seems to be increasing today with the number of tragedies we've had in this country this year alone.

The Psalmist (presumed to be David) goes on to say: "Wait patiently before Him." I am always inspired when people show great patience, compassion and endurance.

Fred Astaire was being interviewed by an MGM Executive. After the audition, he was told that he couldn't act, and that there was no real future in his dancing. Fred was advised to go into another field.

Michael Jordan is 50 years old now but is still considered to be one of the greatest basketball players of all time. But did you know that he didn't make the team when he was in the tenth grade?

Caruso's parents wanted him to be an engineer because his teacher said he couldn't sing.

Walt Disney was fired once because a newspaper editor said he lacked ideas.

Henry Ford went broke five times before he became a success.

Albert Einstein couldn't talk until he was four, and he couldn't read until he was seven. He was classified as being mentally slow.

Finally, look at the Pilgrims who came over on the Mayflower from England. The ship carried 102 people who were seeking a place where they could freely practice their faith. The trip lasted 66 days in the worst of conditions. The first winter was brutal and most remained on the ship, where they suffered exposure, scurvy and other diseases. About a half of them survived to celebrate the First Thanksgiving in 1621. They wouldn't give up nor give in. They were grateful to God, despite everything.

So, whatever it is that gets you down or upsets you terribly, refuse to let it have enough power over you, enough to make you depressed, enough to make you lose hope, enough to make you lose the joy of living. Believe in yourself and hold on to your dreams, even when it's easier to let go. Accept what IS, and stop feeling sorry for yourself, knowing that this world will offer you nothing of lasting value.

Here's hoping this quote from William Shakespeare, "Sweet are the uses of adversity," will one day make the grade of being a familiar cliché. Amen.

WRITING YOUR OWN EPITAPH

I'm not a serious epitaph collector, but I've been to so many cemeteries across this bayou state that I find myself reading the words on tombstones. I've seen some epitaphs that are very revealing about the deceased, and I've also read many that give no clue as to who is buried there other than a name and two dates.

But first, let me tell you about a grave in a London cemetery where John Wesley is buried. I walked around and found the grave of Isaac Watts. "Here Lies Isaac Watts" were the only words there. This had to be the work of a committee.

I smile when I think of the woman who had these words inscribed on her own tombstone: "To Know Her Was To Love Her." No doubt she had high self-esteem.How will you be remembered? What kind of impact are you making? What would you put on your own tombstone? Here are a few Epitaphs that I've found interesting.

1. "He sought the gas leak."
2. This is what someone put on Karen Carpenter's grave: "A star on Earth—a star in Heaven."
3. I like the epitaph on the John Rose family crypt: "This grave's a bed of roses."
4. And, of course, most of have heard about the words on a hypochondriac's stone: "I told you I was sick."

Words on a tombstone can cast a permanent spell over the deceased. Of course, no epitaph could say it all, but they can be insightful. It was William Shakespeare who said, "The evil men do lives after them, the good is oft interred with their bones." Epitaphs can reinforce one or the other.

Consider the implications of this one:

"He always over-ate.
Loving pork and sausage and beef,
He usually scraped his plate;
Thus digging his grave with his teeth." (anon)

One of the people who greatly influenced my life was our minister when I was in my teens. Brother Hugh Castles would almost put you to sleep when preaching, and a group of us used to bet on how many "uhs" he would say in one sermon. And as the old saying goes, he couldn't preach his way out of a paper bag. But Brother Hugh was kind, and friendly, and showed a personal interest in people and their struggles. I don't know what is on his tombstone but it could very well be: "Here lies a wonderfully kind and loving man."

Matthew's Gospel tells about a woman who came with a jar of expensive ointment and poured it on Jesus' head as part of the preparation for burial. When the disciples saw it, they were indignant, saying, "Why this waste? For this ointment could have been sold for a large sum of money and given to the poor." But Jesus defended her: "Why do you trouble the woman, for she has done a beautiful thing to me?" Deeds that are loving and kind are never wasted and Jesus pointed out that she would be remembered for her thoughtfulness. "She did loving deeds" could very well have graced her tombstone. (Mark 14: 3-9)

But the thing I want to emphasize in this article is that it doesn't matter a great deal what words we leave on stones. We live our epitaphs from day to day by the words we speak and the way we treat each other. When the woman came with her perfume, she was criticized. People were against it. The important thing is not what we are against but what we are for. Will future generations be helped or hindered by what we are doing today? We are writing our epitaphs each day.

Let me close on a lighter note. Valentine's Day is coming up. Heaven help us if we are like the man who had these words placed on his wife's tombstone:

"This spot is the sweetest
I've seen in my life
For it raises my flowers
And covers my wife."

If you have a spouse, for goodness sake, please cover him or her with flowers while they're still living. Amen.

LOVE HEALS WHEN NOTHING ELSE WILL

I believe LOVE (unselfish giving) is the greatest healing agent in the world. It's probably the only thing that can heal our messiness. The Scripture says that love is the nature of God, so when we love, we are part of God. For "In Him we live, and move and have our being."

God emptied Himself into human form in the person of Jesus. The Bible tells us that we are heirs of God, and joint heirs with Christ. (Rom. 8:17) If this is true, then we need to celebrate the sacredness of human nature, for each of us is an extension of God's Spirit. This may be the ONLY thing that will stop bullets, and "rumors" of wars.

Love may not be able to heal a tumor or Alzheimer's or cure cancer (that's debatable) but it can heal those who have it. It can take away fear. Love helps us to say "yes" to life. And when we do that, we accept the cycle of life and death, pain and comfort, the mountaintop experiences as well as the dark valleys. When we resist what IS, we set ourselves up for deep disappointments and heartache. We think we are entitled to be pain-free.

Emotional pain can be the deepest pain of all. For instance, when you lose a spouse after 50 years of a happy marriage, you feel that your world caves in and your grief is like a "wound" that takes forever to heal, if it ever does so. You don't expect to get over it, you just get beyond it, and realize that life is still yours to live, and you just may or may not find happiness again. (I'm one of those who are very blessed. I found happiness with another wonderful person in a second marriage and this has brought "healing" in many ways.)

Love never dies a natural death; it has to be killed. And it can be killed in a number of small ways, such as finding fault, unfair criticism, bickering, neglect and a hundred more ways. I believe all of us should memorize the words of St. Paul in I Corinthians: "Love is patient and kind, it is not jealous or boastful, it is not arrogant or rude. It does not insist in having its own way."

Love gives us eyes of the heart. In other words, it helps us to see the needs of the other person and it helps us to love that person for who they ARE, not just what they can do for us. It helps us to appreciate the little things in nature. One spring, I sat on my back porch watching a brown thrash taking worms to her little ones in the bush. It seems that love is built into the very nature of creation.

Someone said, "The number one sin is to judge harshly." That may be true, but I believe the number one sin is to take another person's life. Judging someone harshly is no doubt the forerunner of killing. It's easy to judge another person if they don't believe as we believe, or vote like we vote, or look like we want them to look. Love helps us to see people in a different light. John's Gospel put it this way: "How can we love God whom you have not seen unless you love your brother or sister whom you have seen?"

People in this country are debating gun control issues. It's complicated and nothing assures us that violence will be controlled soon. But isn't this a spiritual issue? A gun doesn't pull its own trigger. It's a people problem, not a gun problem. Consider these Biblical words: "Hatred stirs up trouble, but love covers all sins" (Prov. 10:12) or, "There is no fear in love, but perfect love cast out fear." (I John 4:18) We have become a violent nation because of fear and other negative factors.

Dr. Martin Luther King was right when he said that the only thing that will save this love-starved world is non-violence, and respecting the sacredness of human beings. Amen and Amen.

> For those who are married: "Don't let your love lose its luster—keep dating each other."

ENJOYING THE
SECOND HALF OF LIFE
(Part I)

I was in Lake Charles recently to baptize a great-granddaughter of a church I served in the 70s. After the worship service, a former parishioner came up to me and said, "It's amazing, just amazing." "What's amazing?" I asked. "That you are still alive!" She exclaimed.

It's not only "amazing" but wonderful, because I am alive and grateful that I have lived long enough to see my great-grandchildren; long enough to travel in 12 countries and long enough to have a loving family, plus much, much more.

The second half of life can be good, but sometimes a little scary, because it seems to go so much faster than the first half. There are also many "sink-holes" and things left undone. Jesus must have felt the stress of incompletion because his ministry was cut so short. The second half of life begins somewhere in the late 40s and early 50s, depending on the individual's lifestyle and health. But numbers don't tell the whole story, because some people are old at 40 while others may still be young at 80. It's not only a calendar thing. So much depends upon positive attitudes, and a healthy lifestyle. People who take the high road may not live any longer but they live happier.

I heard about an older man who was creeping along, stooped, grey-haired and a little shaky. A sociology student was interviewing older people for a paper on "longevity." "Pardon me, sir," said the student, "I'd like to ask you a couple of questions for a term paper I'm writing." "Shoot," said the old man. "What is your secret for longevity?" "Well, uh, I eat nothing but junk food, and I booze it up and carouse all night." "Amazing," said the student, "and how old are you?" "Twenty-nine," came the answer.

Although there may come a time when you look in the mirror and see wrinkles never before noticed, bags under your eyes and an unnecessary lump under your chin, you can still have a young outlook on life that carries you right to the end. Trying to hold on to youth is a universal struggle. Being bald didn't appeal to me so I had a hair transplant. It was a little embarrassing to stand in the pulpit with my head all bandaged. I explained it to the congregation and asked them to join me in praying for a "good harvest"

Here are a few thought on how to enjoy the second-half of life:

Stay involved as long as you can. I know from experience that it's tempting to withdraw from certain activities because it takes effort to dress up and go. But I remember the advice an older man gave me one day: "The more involved you are, the more alive you are."

Stay in shape. Live your own life rather than watching others live it. Don't let the TV hold you captive. What we do wrong in the first half of life shows up in the second half. I know a man who started jogging every day but he finally gave it up and said, "My grandfather lived to be 95 and he never jogged a step in his life." We can't go by what our grandparents did or didn't do, because this is a whole new ball game. By the way, I've never seen an obese 90-year-old.

In I Corinthians 3:16-17, we have some pertinent words from the Apostle Paul: "Do you know that you are God's temple and that God's Spirit dwells in you, for God's temple is holy and that you are." Okay, so if I am God's temple I am responsible for what I put into my body and how I treat it. There's a lot confusion about what is good for you. What was bad for you last year, is good for you this year. I real labels and try to stay with a low-fat diet and I look for the expiration dates. My daughter Cindy keeps me "on my toes" concerning expiration dates.

Keep growing in retirement. A rut is a shallow grave. Mend your fences, ask for forgiveness from those you may have hurt. Be non-judgmental. Older people also have a tendency to talk too much. Some folks go off and leave their mouth running. Don't retire too soon. Studies have been made with people who retire at a young age and they die prematurely. I believe your body will tell you when it's time to retire. It worked for me. I retired 8 times. My body finally gave me the message.

Stay in tune spiritually. Jesus said it was necessary to lose one's life in order to find it. The Greeks use two words, both of which we translate by the same word, "life." The first is *psyche*—the biological life studied by science. The other is *zoe*—the transcendent life; the life of God. What kills certain retired people is not a threat from the outside, but from a drama and conflict within. They have a war going on in their own soul and aren't able to accept sickness, loss, old age, dependence or death. Keeping a strong faith and a positive attitude will help you go through all the passages of life.

I began this column with the words of a former parishioner who was amazed that I am still alive. Later, when I told this to a friend, he said this is what I should have said: "Lady, I'm just hanging around so I can officiate at your funeral." Amen.

ENJOYING THE
SECOND HALF OF LIFE
(Part II)

A friend said he grabbed life by the horns, and got gored a couple of times. I think 1 know how he feels. Gored or not, Medical Science tells us that the human body can go well beyond 100, depending upon our life-style, of course. What we do in the first half of life shows up in the second half. Good or bad, we reap what we sow. That's an old law that we can depend upon. This familiar saying has a legitimate point: "If I had known I was going to live this long, I would have taken better care of myself."

Our bodies are "temples of God," as the Apostle Paul wrote in I Corinthians 3:16-17. A major part of spirituality is to take good care of these gifts.

I believe it is God's Will that we live a happy and useful life as long as we can. I am told that "centenarians" are the fastest growing segment of our population. But living to a hundred and above can be punishment unless we live in harmony with the body, mind, and spirit.

If we can get through the mid-life "crazies," as it is sometimes called, the second half should be a little easier. Mid-life is also called the crossroads of life. This is the time when our bodies change, and many go against their own values, and have "flings" or "affairs" in order to prove something. C. S. Lewis once wrote, "There is a shadow side of me that bothers me and is itching to express itself." (A lot of folks scratch where it itches.)

I believe all of us can have peace of mind, but it's tempting to chase rainbows of success, power, prestige and the approval others. We look for it as Ponce de Leon looked for the fountain of youth. We look for it in pills, alcohol or whatever. The last place we look is within the center of our being and we fail to realize that happiness has always been an inside job.

Having said all of this, let's look at a few more ways we can enjoy the second half of life.

1. **Make peace with your limitations**. I heard a woman say, "One of the happiest days of my life was when I accepted the fact that I would never win a beauty contest." If we don't accept our limitations, we can make ourselves very miserable.

2. **Start enjoying a simpler life**. I recommend the book *Blue Zones* by Dan Buettner. He studied 5 different cultures in various parts of the world where there is a large number of centenarians, and many who live to be 100 plus. In Sardinia, Italy, one woman had made it to 122. She said her secret was a sense of humor, olive oil, and port wine. In all five of these places, Buettner concludes that each has a unique path to longevity, showing how their history, traditions, and genes have produced centenarians, and that each one revealed people interacting with each other, shedding stress, healing themselves and having an upbeat attitude toward the world. He also said faith in God and worshipping played a major role.

3. **Moderation in all things**. My late father-in-law had one main sermon: have moderation in everything you do. It's the "extremes" that get us into big trouble .The longer I live, the more I realize his point.

4. **Find your purpose in life**. Someone said if we could find the "why" of life, we could put up with almost any "what" or "how."

5. **Eat until you are no longer hungry rather than eating until you are full**. I've tried it and it does make a difference. A big difference.

6. **Exercise the brain**. Have something to get out of bed for. Learn a new language or take up a musical instrument. Create a personal mission statement. Finish the sentence, "This is what I want to get out of the rest of my life: _____."

7. **Take time to meditate and pray**. A thankful heart is seldom an unhappy heart. "Be still and know that God is God." Said the Psalmist.

8. **Learn to let go**. All of our losses don't come at one time, thank goodness. But they do come. We lose parents, siblings, grand-parents, spouses, etc. The main downside to a long life is outliving people you love. It's the hardest thing we have to do, by far. We were in Shreveport recently and I ran into an old friend, William "Wishy" Nolan, a retired minister. He gave me a book he had just written and I will quote the prologue.

"Lord, help me to hold tight and to let go at the same time.
To release my fears,
To hold on to faith.
To dump my gripes,
And hold to my joys.

To let go of petty things,
To hold to great things.
To release loved ones,
To hold to memories.
Lord, help me to hold to and let go all at the same time."
Amen.

WHAT'S IT LIKE BEING
A PREACHER?

Have you ever wondered what it's like being a preacher?

I cannot speak for all preachers, but let share these thoughts with you.

Being a preacher is being loved and unloved, understood and misunderstood. It is joy and sadness. It is heaven, and to be sure, at times a bit of hell. It is wishing a little girl, "Happy Birthday!" and then rushing off to a funeral.

My profession has kept me in touch with birth and death, love and hate. It has many extremes. It is talking with an alcoholic one minute and counseling a beauty queen the next.

Being a preacher is like going on an African safari with a water gun. It is running into problems that I cannot fix. It is going to a hospital and wondering how much or how little I can be of help. It is standing by a grave, hoping God will touch those whose hearts are broken.

What's it like being a preacher? It is uniting a young couple in marriage and then counseling that SAME couple seven months later. It is going from marriage to the divorce court in the swing of a door. It is offering hope when there is none.

It is twelve hours a day, and sometimes much longer, and "on call" around the clock. It is constantly studying for more sermons, ideas, illustrations and ways to communicate the good news. It is a feeling of inadequacy when you stand in the pulpit and look at hundreds of people who expect to hear some Word from God.

The heartaches and sorrows can certainly overwhelm us as shepherds of the flock. Being a preacher is helping people to live and then helping them to die. And then trying to say something to comfort their loved ones.

It is taking a day off to rest and relax and hearing someone say, "Boy, I wish I had a job where I worked just ONE day a week."

Being a preacher is a high calling, but the person who assumes this role is not much different from anyone else. We bleed. We become impatient, bored and sinful. Sometimes we have ungodly thoughts.

But personally, I wouldn't trade it for any profession in the world.

KEEPING CENTERED—
KEEPING SANE

Life today is much like the tightrope walkers at the circus. You have to stay centered or down you go. Sometimes we are caught between what we'd like to do and what we know we should do. Life is so complicated today and our choices are so many that it's really hard to keep our balance. Those who live without boundaries can, like Humpty Dumpty, have a great fall.

Being centered is the ability to meet the stresses of life without falling apart. It is inner calmness during the storm. We are victims of information overload. It is said the information in one issue of the New York Times is more than the amount taken in by the average person in the entire 17th century.

Thomas Kelly, an outstanding Quaker, described our center as the inner sanctuary of the soul. It is the quiet place where you feel safe or in balance with your surroundings and the people in your life.

I remember a woman who was part of a congregation I served in South Louisiana. When she was in her thirties something traumatic happened to her that destroyed her self-confidence, her self- esteem and her ability to interact with the outside world. She never left her house after that. Relatives had to bring her food, etc. She just couldn't function in a normal way. She lived forty more years as a kind of recluse.

It is said that mental illness is definitely on the increase today. This is evidenced by the number of shootings across the country. It's no shame to be mentally ill, but it is shameful to do nothing about it. Many families tend to ignore a family member who has a pattern of mental illness.

In Elizabeth Brown's book, *Living Successfully with Screwed up People*, are these words: "Relationships with screwed up people are like dancing with porcupines. You want to dance close enough to stay in the waltz, but not so close you end up shot full of quills." Difficult people can threaten your sanity and drive you to your knees. You pray for extra strength and patience. Extra

Strength Tylenol is not strong enough. I know people who remain in toxic and neurotic relationships because they more comfortable with familiar "hells" than with a strange new "heaven."

It has been proven that meditation and getting centered helps people function better in life. Keeping centered is not just to keep us sane. We need to be sane for a reason. We need to be actively involved in making where we are a peaceful and better place.

I'm sure there are many approaches to getting centered but the following steps and thoughts work for me.

1. **Set your goal or ideal**. To connect with God's Spirit within us, remind yourself that you are a spirit with a body, not a body with a spirit. The goal may be to become more forgiving, and loving. Or it may be to overcome resentments, negative attitudes, fear, worry or self-pity. Think about those qualities in your life that you would like to improve.

2. **Set your time**: Start with 10 minutes of silence, reflection. Many like to meditate after that first cup of coffee in the morning. Be consistent whatever time you choose.

3. **Obstacles to meditation**. Refusing to try it; expecting too much too soon. Thinking something big will happen. Not allowing the Spirit of God to come in.

4. **Benefits**: letting your mind and spirit rest. Feeling God's presence not merely on the intellectual level but allowing yourself to be healed of negative thoughts. Realize that the greatest healing is not always physical, but being at peace with yourself, others and with the God of all Creation. Realize that when everything is gone, God is at the center and the center is all we have when we die. The center is the Soul.

5. **True meditation is an active, not a passive art**. It is communion with the deepest, most powerful, most loving and patient part within us. It is more than mumbling a mantra or staring at a candle. It ushers in the HIGHER SELF, that part of us that we would like TO BE and become. The HIGHER self is the opposite of greed, hate, self-pity, narcissism, or "what's in it for me?" Meditation prizes intelligence. It is pragmatic in its purpose, not merely theories, or rituals. It places a high value on the responsibility of the individual to contribute to society.

6. **The purpose of meditation** is to establish better communication between the personality and the higher self. The Higher Self (the BEST part of you) will interact more effectively with others. The purpose of meditation is to heal the person of all negativity. You become easier to live with and you are less judgmental, critical, and self-centered.

7. **Preparation**: Get comfortable, take a few deep breaths, feet flat on the floor. Some put their hands on their knees with palms up, signifying readiness to receive.

8. **Affirmation**: Remind yourself that you are a child of God and you have a right to be here. And you are a special part of creation. I like one or more of these affirmations: "In God's love is my peace," "I can do all things through Him who strengthens me," "The Lord is my shepherd, I shall not want," "God is my refuge and strength, a very present help in time of trouble." There are many positive affirmations.

9. **Concentrate 10 or 15 minutes on your affirmation**. If your mind wanders, bring it back. Your affirmation not only cleanses the mind, it helps you reach the goal. Amen.

HAPPINESS IS ONLY REAL
WHEN SHARED

Christopher McCandless, a young American from Georgia, abandoned the life of comfort to pursue the freedom of life on the road. He burned his credit cards and set out to the Alaskan wilderness, and the challenge of surviving without any modern-day conveniences. A movie, *Into The Wild*, was made from his adventure. About two years later, his body was found in an old abandoned bus in Alaska, plus his diary. These words were highlighted toward the end of his comments: "Happiness is only real when shared."

He thought he could find true happiness going it alone with no strings attached. But it didn't happen for him. It's rare for anyone to thrive in isolation. People need people.

"It is not good for man to be alone." (Genesis 2:18) It seems to me that the truly happy person is un-self-centered, and follows the path of servanthood. The most miserable people I've met are those who are all wrapped up in themselves, asking, "Who will please me, or serve, or meet my needs?" rather than, "How can I serve and help someone else?" Happiness is coming toward the end of life knowing that you've added something good or constructive to life.

Joseph Addison said happiness is something to do, someone to love, and something to hope for.

I cannot reduce "true happiness" to a few words, but if I could, it would have to include enjoying good relationships.

Life does need to be shared. It's a wonderful thing when you can find someone who can help you feel like a "whole" person. Perhaps this is what marriage is all about.

I believe that there are certain building blocks that make for "healthy relationships."

1. RESPECT the rights of the other person. LISTEN for what the other person feels.
2. ACCEPT personal responsibility for your behavior. We have a right as humans to make mistakes as long as we recognize it and learn from it, and seek to change.
3. BE WILLING to admit it when you're wrong. Finding a compromise is important. Saying "I'm sorry" can do wonders for any relationship.
4. ALLOW others to bear the consequences of their own behavior. Caring without enabling a person to continue negative behavior is important
5. STOP the habit of obsessing. You may be obsessing about someone to change their behavior and you may want to rescue them. Reality may not be the way you want it. And you may feel that you are responsible in bringing about change in someone or something. Lighten up on yourself. You can only change yourself.
6. SEE the other person as child of God. PRAY for that person. This can work miracles.

Many times, relationships have great beginnings but turn "toxic" over time. Turning a toxic relationship into a healthy one takes hard work and the setting of new goals. You may love someone who is in trouble, or out of control. It may be emotional, an eating disorder, gambling, alcoholism, or any number of "-isms." Or you may be dealing with someone who is simply difficult. You are embarrassed and humiliated because they are demanding and unreasonable. It takes a lot of courage to GET OUT of a relationship that turns toxic. Also, it takes prayer, and lots of patience. I do not believe God expects us to stay in an abusive, dysfunctional relationship.

One of the greatest enemies to a good relationship is a lack of self-awareness. We can be so narcissistic that we can't see beyond our pattern of behavior. In counseling sessions, a person will often say to me, "There's nothing wrong with me," Or, "this is the way I've always been." Soul searching honesty is the only way I know to remedy this. Getting the selfish ego out of the way can be painful but it can help you to make progress in being the person others enjoy having around.

And now, here are a few "HAPPINESS IS…" one liners.
Happiness is knowing that you don't have to please others all the time.
Happiness is when the Democrats and Republicans work together.
Happiness is when vegetarians eat animal crackers.
Happiness is loving God with all your heart, and soul and strength.
Happiness is going to bed at night with a clear conscience.
Happiness is at least 3 things to look forward to, and nothing to dread.

I believe Lord Byron had it right when he said: "All who find joy must share it, for happiness was born a twin." Amen.

FROM THE AUTHOR

I hope you have enjoyed "Living Faithfully in the Age of Terror."

For similar essay-devotionals, please go to CENLAFOCUS.com, and then click on "FAITH".

Thank you,
Henry C. Blount, Jr. D.Min
henrycblount@gmail.com

CPSIA information can be obtained at www.ICGtesting.com
Printed in the USA
LVOW04s1256020715

444735LV00026B/162/P

9 781480 911321